MONOPOLY
LONDON

The Monopoly Player's Tour of London

Written by Stephen Essberger

MONOPOLY LONDON

Jointly published by Chameleon Publishing and Fotobank Books Ltd.
in association with the English Tourist Board

Great care has been taken to ensure that all factual information contained in this book is accurate. Any errors which appear are the responsibility of the Publisher and not that of the English Tourist Board. Any opinions or subjective views are those of the Author and do not necessarily reflect the opinion or policy of the Publisher or the English Tourist Board.

ISBN 1 869911 02 4

Production Directors: Brian Goodall, Ray Daffurn
Art Director: Andrew Fenton
Designers: John Aspinall, Simon Cheshire
Artwork: Michael Cloke, Lee Marshall, Andrew Saby
Picture Research: Susie Thompson, Stephen Essberger, Ray Daffurn, and John Easterby

Contributors
Visionbank Library Limited
Valuations by Kemsley, Whitely & Ferris
Cartography by kind permission of the English Tourist Board and
Arka Cartographics Limited

Typesetting by Chameleon Graphic Design
Film Repro by Hong Kong Graphic Arts
Printed in Hong Kong by Lee Fung Asco

List of contents

MONOPOLY

Foreword

Monopoly was invented over fifty years ago and has become part of our heritage. As with other great games, one never knows what will happen next. Both luck and skill are needed for victory. The players pit their wits against each other. A faint-hearted player hardly ever wins.

I am often asked how the places on the Monopoly board got their names. The American game is based on the streets of Atlantic City, the seaside resort next to Philadelphia which was the home of the inventor Charles Darrow. Atlantic City is one of the few American cities with names instead of numbers. When my grandfather acquired the rights to publish Monopoly in Britain, it seemed to him to be the most logical and sensible thing to base it on London. He chose well known places but they have become a great deal more famous thanks to Monopoly.

But perhaps, most of all, the magic of Monopoly springs from the city on which the game is based. Many is the time that a visitor to London has cried, "Oh, look! We're in Piccadilly. It's on the Monopoly board." The stranger feels at home; he is in a familiar and friendly place.

VICTOR H WATSON

Author's introduction

The magic of Monopoly and the mystery of London always seemed to me to form an irresistible combination. The evocative names that reverberated around the board had a poetry all their own: Old Kent Road and The Angel Islington, Pall Mall and Marylebone Station, Piccadilly and Mayfair – these were real names in an unreal world. Even the fictitious Community Chest, Electric Company and Super Tax acquired an impenetrable existence of their own.

Together, the streets of London lent the Monopoly board a universal authenticity. Yet by their inclusion these oddly juxtaposed names themselves assumed still greater significance. *Monopoly London* sets out to tour these streets, to discover the origins of their curious names, to uncover their histories, their places of interest and their famous residents. For the reader's convenience the book is essentially split into two parts: Part 1 is a Tour, to be read alike on the ground or in the armchair; Part 2 contains practical Routes to help readers who intend to travel the board in person.

No book on London can be exhaustive, and certainly this one does not attempt to be, even within the confines of the Monopoly board. Rather it is a personal selection in which I have tried to capture the spirit of each street. As a result, errors of omission are on the whole deliberate. Errors of commission, on the other hand, are not. Despite assistance in the vetting of details, to me alone must any lingering blunders be attributed.

Among those to whom the publishers and I are indebted for information, advice and help are: Terry Barringer of the Royal Commonwealth Society; Michael Blakemore of the York Railway Museum; Norman Cochrane; Claire Daunton; Enid Dixon of Westminster Abbey Library; Stephen Eccles and Andy Lickfold of British Rail; Richard Essberger; Major Jenty Fairbank of the Salvation Army; Nancy Fowler; His Grace the Duke of Grafton and Patricia Hamilton, his secretary; Sarah Hepworth; Ann Hewett of the London Electricity Board; George Hoare of the Theatre Royal Drury Lane; John Hoskins; Isabel Hughes of the Livesey Museum; Julie Huntingdon of the Thames Water Authority; Patrick Jiggins; Hugh Kemsley of Kemsley, Whitely & Ferris – chartered surveyors; Isabelle King of the Whitechapel Art Gallery; Stefania Kossowski; Peter Lampert; John Litton; Gavin Morgan and Elizabeth Bannan of the Museum of London; PC Michael Pearse; David Potter; Peter Powell; Judith Prendergast and Elizabeth Mends of the the National Portrait Gallery; Richard Sharp and Paul Williams of the Metropolitan Police Museums; Sheila Taylor of the London Transport Museum; Christopher Slee; Joyce Weddle; Jon Wenzel of the Cabinet War Rooms; the *Daily Telegraph*; the Sherlock Holmes Society of London; and the *Sunday Times Magazine*. Thanks are also due to the Staff of numerous libraries and museums, especially those of: the BBC Hulton Picture Library; the British Library; Guildhall Library; Huntingdon Library; the Imperial War Museum; the Museum of London; the National Gallery; the Post Office Archives; the Public Records Office; Southwark Local Studies Library; and Westminster Central Reference Library.

Special thanks go to William Richards of the English Tourist Board and his colleagues Tessa Williams, whose scrutiny of and comments on the draft text were invaluable, and Susie Thompson, who located so effectively the many historical images; and Ylva French of the London Tourist Board who made many helpful suggestions.

I would also add my personal gratitude for the support of Andrew Fenton and Brian Goodall of Chameleon Publishing, who inspired me throughout this project; for the involvement of Ray Daffurn of Visionbank and for the skill and flair of all at Chameleon Graphic Design who planned and prepared the final layouts. I am indebted to Bridget Lewin for secretarial and research assistance; to my mother, Mary Essberger, for much advice and information; and not least to my wife Tara.

Throughout this book the following conventions have been adopted.

Measurements are shown in metric. (Hectare, which is approximately two acres and a half, is abbreviated as ha.)

Points of interest on, very close to or in some special way related to the Monopoly street in question are marked thus:

point of interest which is usually open to the public.

point of interest which may no longer exist or which may be closed to the public (and entitled to privacy).

Street-numbers are indicated thus #. (Old street-numbers do not necessarily coincide with modern ones.)

From BOARDWALK to MAYFAIR

Black Tuesday for the New York Stock Exchange fell on 29 October 1929. Throughout the 1920s the USA had enjoyed an unprecedented economic boom, with stock values in New York's Wall Street – nerve-centre for the US economy – achieving record levels. Yet late in 1929 Wall Street crashed following the trading of 16,410,030 shares in a single day – wiping 30.57 points off the Dow Jones industrial average and making bankrupts of millionaires. This financial quake reverberated around the globe, triggering aneconomic slump in most of the industrialized world that lasted until 1939. Inthe USA alone, security values plunged $74,000,000,000 within three years and one out of every four workers was rendered jobless.

125km south-west of the New York Stock Exchange, in Philadelphia, Pennsylvania – itself a major banking centre – a forty-year old salesman was one of those thrown out of work. In the bitter chill of the Great Depression the heating equipment that Charles B Darrow supplied seemed redundant.

Almost 100km to the south-east lay the Atlantic Ocean, its waters tempered by the warmth of the Gulf Stream. Here, less than a century before, a visiting doctor had encouraged the founding of a seaside idyll. By the boom days of the 1920s Atlantic City was a fashionable health resort linked by railroad to Philadelphia. Grand hotels lined the sea-front. Amusement piers jutted into the ocean from the stylish, beach-side Boardwalk. Vendors, fairs and exhibitors maintained an atmosphere of ceaseless carnival. In the heady days before 1929, Charles Darrow and his wife, like countless fellow Americans, vacationed here annually.

Manhattan's 550m Wall Street is home of the vast New York Stock Exchange and pulse of the entire capitalist world.

The New York Stock Exchange is today the greatest and most prestigious in the world, with a market capitalization exceeding $2,000,000,000,000.

Thus was set the scene for the creation of the world's best-selling copyrighted game in history: the Great Depression – widespread bankruptcy – mass unemployment – an out-of-work salesman with a resourceful turn of mind — and happy memories of Atlantic City.

Charles Darrow eked out a living by taking on odd jobs. But he dreamed of true wealth through the invention of games. His simplified bridge scoring-pad and novel bat-and-ball game were commercial failures, yet he persevered. His next invention was a property-trading game in which the streets and railroads were actual names taken from Atlantic City. In it players could buy property, charge rent, erect houses and hotels, mortgage land, pay taxes and interest charges, go to jail – and go bankrupt. The winner achieved a monopoly. MONOPOLY was an instant success. This was a game of events that happened in real life – and life in Depression-torn America was positively unreal. Here was a way to reverse at will the traumas of recent times – the ultimate metaphor for the capitalist way of life so rudely shaken by the Wall Street Crash. Local demand far exceeded supply, but large-scale production of his intoxicating new game eluded Darrow. His gaze turned towards Salem, Massachusetts, on the Atlantic seaboard north of New York.

Proposals in the early-1970s to rename some of the original MONOPOLY streets of this New Jersey coastal-resort-cum-convention-centre created such a nationwide furore that they were ultimately vetoed.

Here was the games capital of the world, home for over half a century of Parker Brothers, largest games manufacturers on earth. In 1934 Parker Brothers were themselves suffering from a depressed market, and they regretfully but unanimously rejected Darrow's MONOPOLY. With its 'fifty-two fundamental errors' it broke all the rules for a family game: it lasted too long; it had no obvious conclusion; it was too complex.

In response, Darrow did everything possible to step up production. By Christmas 1934 he had made 20,000 sets for that year, many of them sold to department stores, at first in Philadelphia, ultimately in New York itself. It soon became clear to Parker Brothers that they had made a serious error of judgement. This time they approached Darrow, and a deal was struck granting him an attractive royalty. By mid-February 1935 Parker Brothers were manufacturing and selling as many MONOPOLY sets each week as Darrow had managed in the whole of 1934. Charles Darrow never regretted his decision: he retired a few years later on the enormous wealth that MONOPOLY brought him. When he died in 1967 he was a multi-millionaire – the world's first millionaire games designer.

The definitive MONOPOLY that Parker Brothers launched nationwide in 1935 had a distinct American flavour. But their new wonder-game was not to remain restricted to the USA for long. Early in 1935 Parker Brothers licensed John Waddington in the United Kingdom to manufacture and market sets in Britain and other parts of the world. Thus it was that the famous London MONOPOLY board came into existence. Together, Victor Watson senior – head of Waddingtons – and his secretary Marjory Phillips converted the Atlantic City board to London. Atlantic City RAILROADs became London railway STATIONs – the locomotives discreetly redesigned without cow-catchers; all streets were renamed so that STATES AVENUE became WHITEHALL – still the bastion of UK government, ORIENTAL AVENUE

London's elegant MAYFAIR Hotel — fitting venue for the 1987 UK MONOPOLY Championship.

became THE ANGEL ISLINGTON – once the archetypal English inn, and fashionable BOARDWALK became blue-blooded MAYFAIR – then a repository of British nobility; LUXURY TAX became SUPER TAX; and US dollars became pounds sterling. Apart from that, little changed. The idiosyncratic design of the board remained intact. So, too, did many of the minor Americanisms. The new board still had its American welfare COMMUNITY CHEST, American spelling for IN JAIL, Edison-screw light bulb, 1930s Plymouth and New York cop. But the flavour was definitely British, with evocative-sounding streets like OLD KENT ROAD, PICCADILLY and the STRAND, and world-famous landmarks like TRAFALGAR SQUARE.

The majority of MONOPOLY London streets occur to the west of St Paul's Cathedral, in the City of Westminster. The 'square mile' to the east is the largest financial centre in the world.

In 1985 Waddingtons issued a 50th anniversary edition of MONOPOLY, its idiosyncratic design barely changed from the original sets that Charles Darrow manufactured a half-century before in Germantown, Philadelphia.

Since then MONOPOLY has become an institution, adapted to many other cities, translated into more than fifteen languages and played by over 250,000,000 people across the globe – sometimes in the strangest circumstances. In 1967 the Great Train Robbers used part of their £2,500,000 haul of bank notes from a British mail train to play MONOPOLY at their Cheddington hide-out. NASA commissioned specially engineered MONOPOLY sets for use by astronauts in space. The American Foundation for the Blind translated MONOPOLY into braille. It has been played underwater, underground, in a lift, in a bath, in prison and beneath the Polar ice cap. It was played by Sir Winston Churchill and by Aristotle Onassis. Every few years a new World MONOPOLY Champion emerges from tense national and international competitions. And it is played covertly in the highest echelons of Communist bloc society – where it is publicly denounced as a 'decadent instrument of imperial capitalism'. Yet since the capitalist crash from which it was born, MONOPOLY has lost none of its universal appeal. Since 1935 Waddingtons alone have manufactured more than 15,000,000 sets and issued over £200,000,000,000. Parker Brothers have manufactured more than 100,000,000 sets; and their daily issue of more than $200,000,000 exceeds the output of the US Treasury – making their annual print-run equivalent to the record value of US securities lost between 1929 and 1932.

PART I

PALL MALL £140
ELECTRIC COMPANY
IN JAIL
PENTONVILLE ROAD £120
EUSTON ROAD £100
CHANCE
THE ANGEL ISLINGTON £100
KINGS CROSS STATION
BRITISH RAILWAYS
£200
PAY £2
THE ANGEL, ISLINGTON
KING'S CROSS
TITLE DEED
BOND STREET
RENT – site only £28
" with 1 house 150
" " 2 houses 450
" " 3 houses 1000
" " 4 houses 1200
" " HOTEL 1400
If a player owns all the sites of any Colour-Group, the rent is doubled on unimproved sites in that group
COST of houses – £200 each
" " hotels – £200 plus 4 houses
MORTGAGE value of site £160
MONOPOLY
500
100
COMMUNITY CHEST
GET OUT OF JAIL FREE
This card may be kept until needed or sold

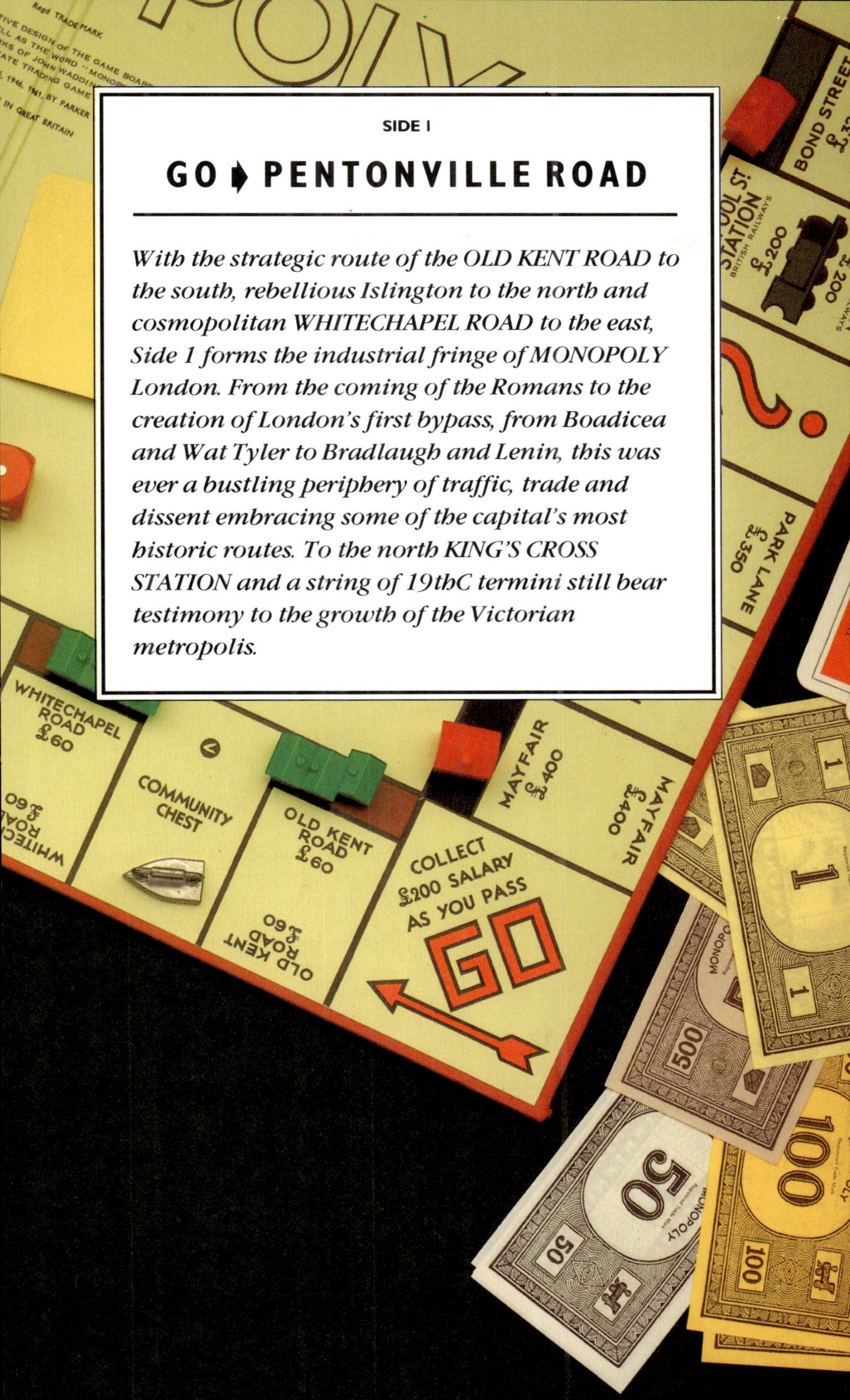

SIDE 1

GO ▶ PENTONVILLE ROAD

With the strategic route of the OLD KENT ROAD to the south, rebellious Islington to the north and cosmopolitan WHITECHAPEL ROAD to the east, Side 1 forms the industrial fringe of MONOPOLY London. From the coming of the Romans to the creation of London's first bypass, from Boadicea and Wat Tyler to Bradlaugh and Lenin, this was ever a bustling periphery of traffic, trade and dissent embracing some of the capital's most historic routes. To the north KING'S CROSS STATION and a string of 19thC termini still bear testimony to the growth of the Victorian metropolis.

GO

The Making of London

'No, Sir, when a man is tired of London, he is tired of life; for there is in London all that life can afford.'

Samuel Johnson (1709-84)

All but one of the streets on the MONOPOLY board lie north of the Thames. Most traverse **Westminster**, avenues of power and political intrigue. Three MONOPOLY spaces infiltrate the **City**, nerve-centre for a world of finance and banking. In reality, these are two Londons – two individual communities which evolved discretely, their identities later engulfed by a ravenous stonescape to which each was at once sire and sacrifice.

Dragons traditionally guard the City of London and have for centuries formed part of its heraldic bearings. This bronze dragon – at the junction of FLEET STREET and STRAND – bestrides Temple Bar Memorial in defence of the modern boundary between the City of London and the City of Westminster.

Claudius I, fourth Roman Emperor, fleetingly visited Britain during the invasion of AD43. On his return to Rome he was honoured with the title 'Britannicus'.

The dome of Sir Christopher Wren's 17thC St Paul's Cathedral still dominates the City of London skyline. The first St Paul's on this site was founded in AD604; the second, larger and taller than Wren's, was started in the 11thC.

GO

Londinium: City of London

When, late in the season of AD43, the Roman general Aulus Plautius invaded Britain with 20,000 legionaries, advancing inland along the route of the OLD KENT ROAD, he crossed a broad, meandering Thames at its lowest convenient bridging point. Here, on twin hills where now stand St Paul's Cathedral and Cornhill, he established Londinium as his base. Here too, in AD61, Boadicea – warrior-queen of the British Iceni tribe – obliterated Londinium in an orgy of revenge in which up to 30,000 Romans and sympathisers were mercilessly butchered. It was a grim convulsion that provoked the Romans to punitive retaliation and the extensive fortification of a rebuilt Londinium – so that by the late-2ndC a massive, 6m high stone wall defined the 3km^2 Roman city, official capital of the province. To this thriving, international port – sixth city of the Roman Empire – came merchant ships from all corners of the known world. Yet when, early in the 5thC, a beleaguered Empire withdrew its last remaining legions from Britain, London found independence thrust upon it. Through the mists of the ensuing Dark Ages, the walled city – at first a derelict ghost-town, later tossed between Viking and Saxon – strove staunchly to maintain its sovereignty.

Alan Sorrell's reconstruction drawing of Roman London about AD100.

Mid-16thC map-view clearly showing the already mature City of London linked by the STRAND to the smaller but developing Westminster (Braun and Hogenberg).

Heat-density (infra-red) satellite map of Greater London taken from an altitude of 700km in 1984. Hyde Park, Heathrow Airport and the M25 orbital motorway are clearly discernible (Landsat).

West Minster: City of Westminster

By the 11thC, friction between Crown and City prompted the godly King Edward the Confessor to move his Court 3km upstream to Thorney Island – site of his imposing new monastery dedicated to St Peter, whose sacred feet, it was whispered, had once trod this very spot. The effect of this transfer was profound, moulding the shape of London ever since: inevitably the monastery or minster to the west of the City became 'Westminster', tiny seat of justice and royal power; while the larger City of London remained the centre of commerce and financial influence.

When, in 1066, William of Normandy conquered Britain, he grudgingly acknowledged the independent status of the City. Ostensibly to protect it from river attack, but in reality perhaps also to overawe its irksome citizens, William embarked upon the construction of his vast and sophisticated riverside fortress – the Tower of London – just at the south-eastern angle of the city wall. Yet his son Rufus and succeeding monarchs lived increasingly at Westminster, inhabiting ever more grandiose and lavish royal palaces like WHITEHALL. The two important communities, whose proximity encouraged ribbon development along the Thames, were early united by a string of elegant mansions along the STRAND.

This then was the stage on which the giants of history were to strut. Lonely kings and perfidious knights, tragic queens and amorous statesmen – all paced a vibrant townscape destined one day to rule the world's most far-flung empire. London prospered – and grew. The City itself, incarcerated within its protective walls, could never really expand outwards: it grew upwards instead, after a fashion. Unconstricted Westminster – already linked to the City by its riverside ligament – blossomed with evocative names like PALL MALL, PICCADILLY, MAYFAIR. Soon it was as large as the City, then larger, with EUSTON ROAD its first bypass. Iron horses stabled at the City's tiny FENCHURCH STREET STATION or Westminster's romantic MARYLEBONE STATION, as outlying villas, farms and communities like THE ANGEL ISLINGTON coalesced within London's inexorable expansion.

The City of London is still a metaphor for high finance.

The Palace of Westminster, symbol of parliamentary democracy – a Victorian fantasy with a thousand-year lineage.

OLD KENT ROAD

(SE1,SE15/London Borough of Southwark)

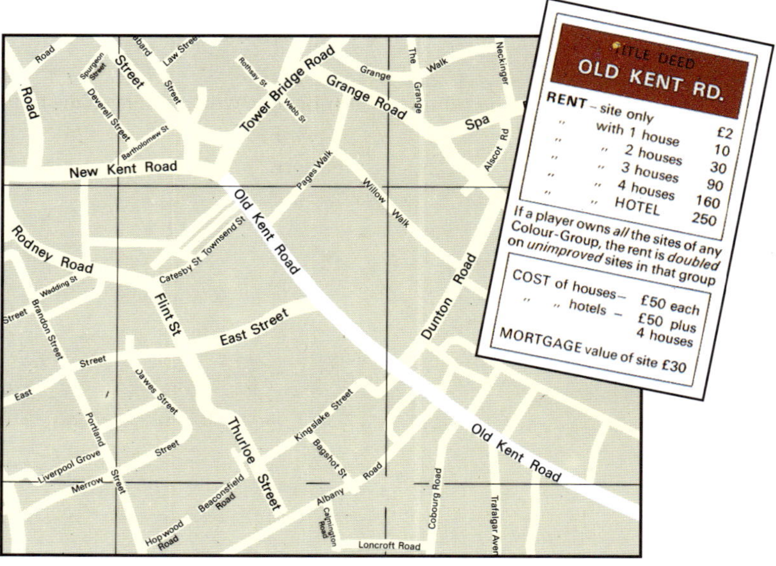

MONOPOLY valuation: £60
Current valuation: £28,125,000

Location description

The OLD KENT ROAD, the only MONOPOLY street south of the River Thames, is appropriately also the first space on the board. For hundreds of years this route was the gateway to London. Along its length could be heard the tramp of hoof and foot as its bustling traffic surged to and from mainland Europe. The OLD KENT ROAD is the longest street on the MONOPOLY board, stretching for more than 3km along the line of old Roman Watling Street, the Dover road heading for Kent, the Channel ports – and the Continent. With changing traffic patterns to and from the coast, the OLD KENT ROAD is slowly losing its strategic significance. Today it is celebrated more for the memory of its Victorian costermongers and flower-sellers than its historic rôle in London's development; but imaginative revamping of its famous pubs and hot-pie and jellied-eel shops has recently given this still busy thoroughfare a new vitality.

Derivation of name

Kent, the south-easternmost county of Britain, is also the oldest place name in England. In the 18thC the whole of the OLD KENT ROAD, which extended further north, was known as Kent Street in reference to its destination. Early-19thC road improvement schemes resulted in the construction at its northern end of a new route called the New Kent Road. The remnant of Kent Street became the OLD KENT ROAD.

Short history

London's original Roman roads are, in many cases, still in use as modern routes. Watling Street approached London from Dover and crossed the Thames at the only bridging-point, London Bridge, which the Romans built within fifteen years of their invasion in AD43. From there it continued its long, straight alignment through the modern Marble Arch and along Edgware Road as it set off again for the important settlement of St Albans. The OLD KENT ROAD grew up on this former Roman route. London Bridge was in fact the City's only river crossing until the 18thC; and the route of the OLD KENT ROAD, linking London to the Channel ports, was therefore of enormous importance for centuries.

For many years the OLD KENT ROAD was known as Kinges Street, and along it passed many royal processions. The Black Prince returned victorious from France along Kinges Street. In 1415 Henry V took this road, returning from victory at Agincourt. In 1522 the Holy Roman Emperor Charles V visited Henry VIII, resting in a 'tent of cloth of gold' along the OLD KENT ROAD. In 1660 a golden armoured Charles II rode this way, returning from exile in Holland to proclaim the restoration of the monarchy. Other, less royal, processions also trod this route. In 1381 the rebellious men of Kent marched along here to London, sacking Lambeth Palace and beheading the Archbishop of Canterbury. In June 1450, having skirmished with and defeated Henry VI's troops at Sevenoaks, 20,000 Kentish men again took this road to London, an insurrection finally repulsed at London Bridge.

Synchronous illustration of the killing of Wat Tyler, leader of the 1381 Peasants' Revolt, followed by an immediate appeal by the teenage King Richard II to the leaderless rebels (*Chroniques de France et d'Angleterre* c1460).

Points of interest

The Thomas à Becket (#320) is a Victorian pub built on the site of St Thomas à Waterings. Here it was that Chaucer's 14thC Canterbury Pilgrims halted on their journey to the shrine of St Thomas à Becket.

'And forth we riden a little more than pas
Unto the Watering of St Thomas –
And there our hosts began his hors' arrest.'

This spot, where a stream crossed the road, was always a meeting point and for several hundred years a place of execution. Today the pub is known for its boxers' training gym and its world-famous museum housing some 1,000 boxing exhibits. Just up the road is another pub with boxing associations: the Henry Cooper. A third tavern, the Drover, recalls the chaos and dust as drovers amused themselves stampeding herds of fat cattle *en route* to London's markets from the pastures of Kent. Dotted with curious names like the World Turned Upside Down and the OLD KENT ROAD Gin Palace, the road has long been famous for its many pubs.

Above: The pearly kings and queens of today echo the traditions of Victorian costermongers.
Right: The present Thomas à Becket was rebuilt in 1898.

Costermongers The Victorian music-hall song *Knocked 'em in the OLD KENT ROAD* by Albert Chevalier recalls the hard-working costermongers whose long-suffering donkeys and fruit-laden barrows lined the street. The OLD KENT ROAD was famous for its street markets of fruit and vegetables brought in from Kent on costermongers' barrows. The word costermonger itself is derived from 'costard' (a large ribbed kind of apple) and 'monger'. From the costers of London came today's spectacular pearly kings and queens, with their suits smothered in dazzling patterns of pearl buttons and their charitable mission to raise money for the poor.

OLD KENT ROAD Mural On two faces of the North Peckham Civic Centre and Library (#168) the Polish artist Adam Kossowski has recreated the history of the OLD KENT ROAD in a vivid mural. Measuring 24m in length and consisting of some 2,000 panels, it is a work of impressive craftsmanship and representation.

The first section of Adam Kossowksi 's OLD KENT ROAD mural is entitled 'Via Romana'.

Camberwell Beauty This beautiful butterfly, found nearby at Camberwell when the area was still rural, is commemorated by Bryan Kneale's graceful steel mobile inside the Civic Centre (#168).

The **Livesey Museum** (#682), opened by Poet Laureate Sir John Betjeman in 1974, houses exhibitions of local interest. The red-brick building was erected in 1890 as Camberwell Public Library Number One, the gift of Sir George Livesey, philanthropic chairman of the nearby South Metropolitan Gas Company.

Famous people

Wat Tyler (d1381) was the legendary leader of the 1381 Kentish peasants' revolt against a newly imposed poll tax. Tyler had struck dead a collector who insulted his daughter. By 12 June nearly 100,000 men had gathered on Blackheath to march on London via the OLD KENT ROAD. Tyler himself was personally slain by the Mayor of London while parleying with the king, Richard II, on 15 June.

Jack Cade (d1450), Irish-born rebel who assumed the name of Mortimer, led the 1450 Kentish insurrection along the OLD KENT ROAD. When a general pardon was announced, a deserted Cade withdrew to Rochester, a price on his head. Scorning surrender, he was killed by the Sheriff of Kent on 11 July.

Charlie Chaplin (1889–1977), internationally acclaimed comic film actor and director, was born near the OLD KENT ROAD of theatrical parents.

Adam Kossowski (1905-1986), Polish sculptor of the OLD KENT ROAD Mural, was educated at the Cracow and Warsaw Academies of Art. Held prisoner in a Russian labour camp from 1939-42, he settled in Britain after the War to specialize in sacred art.

Henry Cooper (b1934), famous British boxer, ex-British, -European and -Commonwealth heavyweight champion, used to train at the gym above the bar of the Thomas à Becket public house in the OLD KENT ROAD.

Above: A young Charles Spencer Chaplin, who was knighted in 1975. Left: Wembley 18 June 1963 – 'Cooper hammers Clay to canvas'.

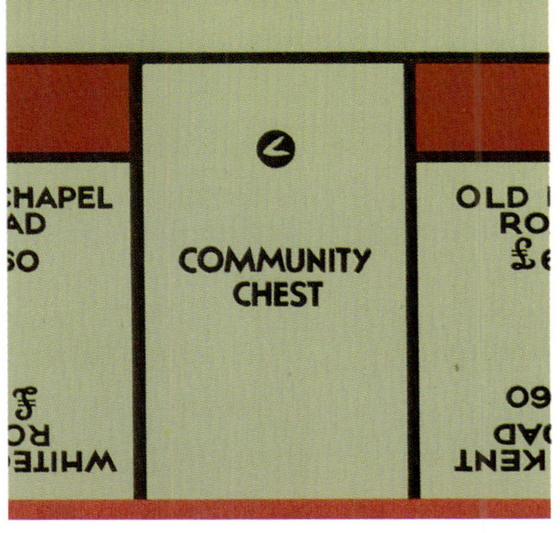

COMMUNITY CHEST

YOU HAVE WON SECOND PRIZE IN A BEAUTY CONTEST COLLECT £10

Did you know . . . that the largest annual beauty contest on earth, Miss World, is staged in London at the Royal Albert Hall, attended by beauty queens from over eighty countries?

BANK ERROR IN YOUR FAVOUR COLLECT £200

Did you know . . . that the Bank of England once replaced a £30,000 banknote lost by one of its directors; and that thirty years later, in 1770, the Bank also had to honour the original note, discovered trapped behind a fireplace in the late director's house?

ADVANCE TO "GO"

Did you know . . . that the former 19thC London Bridge – built near the site of the 1stC Roman bridge – was dismantled and re-erected in 1971 at Lake Havasu City, Arizona, USA at a purchase price of £1,000,000?

ANNUITY MATURES COLLECT £100

Did you know . . . that the City of London – even today an international centre of commerce and high finance – was described in 1904 by British statesman Joseph Chamberlain as 'the clearing-house of the world'?

GO BACK TO OLD KENT ROAD

Did you know . . . that of all the spaces on the MONOPOLY board the route of the OLD KENT ROAD is the first, oldest, longest, least expensive, most easterly and most southerly – and the only one south of the River Thames?

Popular associations: Cockney street-traders / textiles / Jack the Ripper

WHITECHAPEL ROAD

(E1/London Borough of Tower Hamlets)

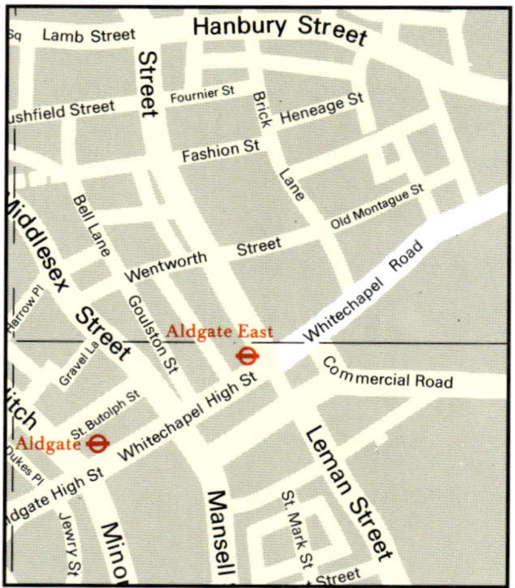

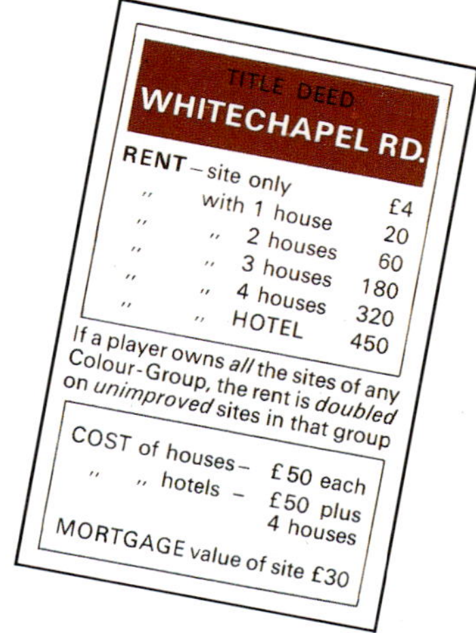

MONOPOLY valuation: £60
Current valuation: £56,250,000

Location description

After the OLD KENT ROAD this street is appropriately the least expensive on the MONOPOLY board. Its broad artery links Whitechapel High Street in the west with Mile End Road in the east. Situated in London's East End, an area of trade and industry where refugees of many races historically found shelter, WHITECHAPEL ROAD is the antithesis of high-society PARK LANE in the west. Today, Asian textile companies and Jewish export houses finance deals through neighbouring Arab banks; gilt-lettered taverns with names like Grave Maurice and Blind Beggar quench Cockney street-traders' thirsts; while Methodist chapels and Muslim mosques summon to prayer a catholic faithful.

Derivation of name

The original chapel from which the area took its name was built of white stone in the 13thC, becoming the church of St Mary Whitechapel c1338.

Short history

By the middle of the 16thC Whitechapel was a small community on the eastern fringes of London, straddling the main route to Essex. It soon grew to accommodate many trades considered a nuisance in the more confined City. Already the inhabitants tended to be impoverished and poorly housed, engaged in metal working industries like gun-making. One 16thC commentator considered the area to be 'no small blemish to so famous a city'. In the following centuries Whitechapel's poverty was not relieved by the settlement here of refugees fleeing persecution in Europe and Russia.

Reaching London by river, and often finding themselves barred as foreigners from entry to the City, these early *émigrés* settled here where they landed. Italians, Huguenots, Jews – and later Asians and Arabs – this is the special blend of cultures that has endowed Whitechapel with its uniquely cosmopolitan atmosphere and vitality.

Early-18thC view of St Mary-le-Bow, Cheapside, whose 'Bow Bells' are both made and heard in WHITECHAPEL ROAD.

Points of interest

The **Whitechapel Bell Foundry** (#32/34), with an unbroken ancestry dating back to 1420, moved to its present site in 1738 and still occupies part of an inn building of c1670. Since 1583 this world-famous foundry has made the bells for Westminster Abbey – as well as for churches in the City, the rest of Britain, the USA and Russia.

Above: Interior of the Whitechapel Bell Foundry.
Left: Marie Jeanette Kelly, probably the Ripper's final victim, was last seen alive leaving this public house – then known as the Ten Bells.

Whitechapel Murders Whitechapel is grimly linked to one of the most macabre of English murder mysteries. All six of the victims generally attributed to Jack the Ripper were slain in the Whitechapel district. His first was discovered in George Yard Buildings on 7 August 1888. Over the next three months the Ripper claimed five more victims: all women; all in an area of one square mile; all but one soliciting prostitutes; all found with throat slashed; and all mutilated with a grim precision that led police to conclude that the murderer had a detailed knowledge of surgery. Despite public outcry and intensive investigation, the Ripper eluded detection. After his final and most revolting murder, on 9 November 1888, he retired into obscurity. To this day the case of the Whitechapel Murders arouses the most intense but so far futile speculation as to his true identity.

Post Office underground railway Opened in 1927, this 9.5km track between Whitechapel and Paddington links six sorting offices, including the massive Mount Pleasant. With its electric trains and daily capacity of 50,000 bags of mail, this is the only railway of its kind in the world.

The original trains of the Post Office underground railway shown here were superseded by thirty-four new ones in the early-1980s.

Booth House (#153/175) is a large Salvation Army hostel for homeless men. The now world-wide Salvation Army, founded by the Reverend William Booth in 1865, was at first called the Christian Revival Association. Its headquarters opened in WHITECHAPEL ROAD in 1867.

The Blind Beggar In the late 1960s London was stunned by a brazen Al Capone-style gangland killing at this pub. This was to be the downfall of its perpetrators, the infamous Kray brothers, each given thirty-year prison sentences in 1968.

The Blind Beggar, a colourful public house typical of London's East End.

Sidney Street, at the junction of WHITECHAPEL ROAD and Mile End Road, would have remained an obscure East End name but for the exploits of two early-20thC burglars. As it was, the 'Siege of Sidney Street' entered the annals of British history on 3 January 1911 when Home Secretary Winston Churchill came to witness the Scots Guards, Horse Artillery and 750 policemen deal with two armed immigrants who had barricaded themselves into #100.

The **London Hospital** (WHITECHAPEL ROAD), founded at Moorfields in 1740 and rebuilt on the green fields of Whitechapel in 1757, is one of the largest general hospitals in England. It was, in its day, the most advanced in Britain, even boasting a crude water-flushing system.

A peaceful **Jewish Cemetery** in Brady Street dating from 1761 contains the tomb of Nathan Meyer Rothschild (d1836), London representative of the famous family of financiers. An 1899 map of London by Charles Booth indicates 29 synagogues in the Whitechapel area and only five elsewhere in London.

Cockneys Many inhabitants of Whitechapel can claim authentic cockney blood. The term, now applied endearingly, came from the word 'cokeney' which meant cock's egg and thus infertile and useless. 17thC countrymen applied it to townspeople, specifically Londoners. Today, an authentic cockney must have been born within the sound of Bow Bells – the peal of bells of St Mary-le-Bow, Cheapside, made here at the bell foundry in WHITECHAPEL ROAD.

The **Whitechapel Art Gallery** (#80/82 Whitechapel High Street), designed in 1899 by Harrison Townsend, is one of Britain's most famous art nouveau buildings. Townsend was a highly original Victorian architect, exponent of the influential arts and crafts movement. The Gallery is internationally respected for its exhibitions of unusual interest.

The Whitechapel Art Gallery gave the first British one-man shows to American artists like Jackson Pollock, Mark Rothco and Philip Guston.

Price Albert Victor (1864-92), Duke of Clarence.

Famous people

Jack the Ripper The true identity of this vicious murderer has never been established or at least revealed. Sir Arthur Conan Doyle, creator of Sherlock Holmes, thought that the Ripper clothed himself as a woman. Other theories have suggested that the Ripper actually was a woman. Possible suspects include: *Montague Druitt,* a teacher who, at 31, filled his pockets with stones and jumped into the Thames shortly after the last murder. After his suicide the police closed their files on the case; *Dr Stanley,* a Harley Street surgeon whose son died of syphilis contracted from Mary Kelly, the Ripper's last victim; *Kominski,* a Polish Jew who 'indulged in solitary vices' and was confined to a lunatic asylum in 1889; *Dr Alexander Pedachenko,* a sinister Russian criminal lunatic allegedly working on behalf of the Russian secret service to embarrass the British police; the *Duke of Clarence,* Queen Victoria's grandson, upon whom suspicion seems to have fallen because of her unusual interest in the case; *Sir William Gull,* the Royal Physician, who, it is proposed, picked up and murdered his victims in a carriage, dumping their bodies later.

Charles Bradlaugh (1833-91), atheist and free thinker, lived at #29 Turner Street. Under the name Iconoclast he promoted his ideas so lucidly that in 1868 he was prosecuted for blasphemy and sedition.

'General' William Booth, founder of the Salvation Army.

William Booth (1829-1912), Methodist preacher, began his missionary work in the Whitechapel area in 1865. From his Whitechapel Mission grew the Salvation Army's now world-wide hostels for down-and-outs.

Charles Booth (1840-1916), wealthy Liverpool shipowner and ardent social reformer, spent all his money researching into the working classes of Whitechapel and other parts of London.

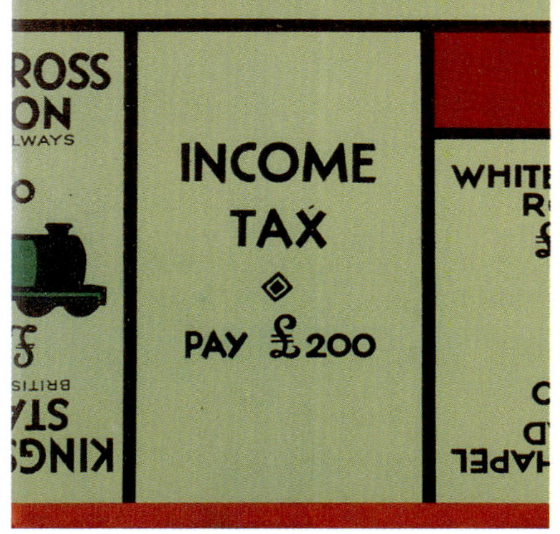

INCOME TAX
PAY £200

The *Concise Oxford Dictionary* defines tax as a 'contribution levied on persons, property or business, for support of national government', adding ominously as a second definition 'oppressive or burdensome obligation'. INCOME TAX might fairly be considered to be both, and the official body responsible for its collection in Britain resides at the very heart of MONOPOLY London.

Total public expenditure in the UK far exceeds £150,000,000,000 annually, most of which is raised by a plethora of taxes. The most successful of these is INCOME TAX, administered and collected by the Board of Inland Revenue from their STRAND headquarters, Somerset House – London's first purpose-built government offices established in 1785. If laid end to end as a line of £1 MONOPOLY notes, the annual yield from INCOME TAX – over £40,000,000,000 – would stretch more than 100 times around the world.

A graduated tax on income – commencing at 2s in the £ (or 10%) on incomes over £60 per annum – was first imposed in Britain in 1799 'as an aid to the prosecution of the war' with Napoleon. Discontinued and subsequently re-imposed, by 1875 the rate had fallen to its lowest ever – 2d in the £ (or 0.83%). Its highest level was achieved during the Second World War at a rate of 10s in the £ (or 50%).

The highest disclosed UK personal INCOME TAX demand was one for over £5,000,000.

From his official residence at #11 Downing Street, the Chancellor of the Exchequer yearly sets off for the House of Commons to present his Budget for the coming year. The secrets of INCOME TAX changes are locked within the historic red despatch box which he traditionally flourishes for the news media.
Top: Some Chancellors need more than one Budget yearly. This was Mr Denis Healey's thirteenth (Tuesday 11.04.78).
Centre: Sir Geoffrey Howe (Tuesday 15.03.83).
Right: Mr Nigel Lawson (Tuesday 19.03.85).

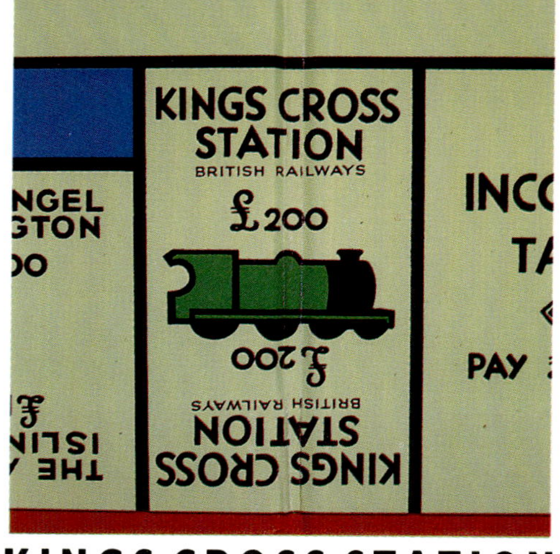

KINGS CROSS STATION

(EUSTON ROAD, NW1/London Borough of Camden)

Principal terminus of British Rail's important East Coast Route to Scotland, KING'S CROSS STATION is the most northerly site on the MONOPOLY board.

MONOPOLY valuation: £200
Current valuation: £236,000,000

Opening date

1852

Principal destinations

Include Aberdeen, Doncaster, Edinburgh, Grimsby, Hull, Leeds, Newcastle, Peterborough and York.

Traffic statistics

Passenger trains daily: 250
Passengers daily: 37,000

Station background

London's railway termini offer an interesting clue to the capital's 19thC growth. South of the Thames development was patchy and the new railways were able to push right into the heart of the city, even crossing the river in some cases; but in the north they were curbed by a more vigorous urban growth. KING'S CROSS STATION is one of a festoon of termini across London's northern 19thC limits.

Erected at a cost of £123,000 in a district previously known as Battle Bridge, KING'S CROSS STATION was designed in 1851-2 by Lewis Cubitt, youngest architect brother of master builder Thomas Cubitt. Its spectacular original frontage demonstrates clearly how aesthetic grace follows functional form. Cubitt was not ashamed to build a station: twin train sheds each 240m long and 32m wide; covered approaches for carriages and carts; all surmounted by a 34m high clock tower. There was no need for elaboration. In Cubitt's words he wanted to achieve 'fitness for its purpose and the characteristic expression of that purpose'. He succeeded magnificently as early illustrations show.

Originally KING'S CROSS STATION was the terminus of the Great Northern Railway with lines to York and the north-east of England. When it opened, spanned by the largest roof in the world, it was the biggest station in England and the fifth to be built in London. By the end of the 19thC KING'S CROSS STATION was servicing about 250 trains daily, just as today.

KING'S CROSS STATION old and new. The classic lines of Cubitt's original design are readily discernible behind the 1973 passenger concourse.

Station timetable

AD62: Boadicea, Queen of the Iceni, defeated by the Romans, allegedly buried somewhere under site now occupied by main departure platform #8.

1830: monument to King George IV erected nearby. From this vast edifice (used first as a police station, then as a pub) King's Cross takes its name.

1852 (14 October): KING'S CROSS STATION opens to traffic.

1854: Cubitt adds 66-bedroom, crescent-shaped Great Northern Hotel.

1914-18 (First World War): main-line trains drawn into station tunnels when enemy aircraft overhead. Terminus plays strategic part in transport of armaments, high explosives and troops.

1921: world's first restaurant car equipped with electric kitchen leaves KING'S CROSS STATION.

1924: first cinema coach leaves KING'S CROSS STATION.

1927: 9.50am KING'S CROSS STATION to Newcastle sets world record of

1928: *Flying Scotsman* makes world record non-stop run of 633km from KING'S CROSS STATION to Edinburgh.

1934: Brighton Trunk Murder stuns nation. Severed legs found at KING'S CROSS STATION match naked female torso discovered at Brighton Station. Identities of victim and culprit unknown.

1935: *Silver Jubilee,* Britain's first streamlined locomotive, departs from KING'S CROSS STATION.

1937: *Coronation* brings KING'S CROSS STATION and Edinburgh within six hours of each other.

1939-45 (Second World War): severe damage and loss of life inflicted at KING'S CROSS STATION by two 1000lb bombs chained together. Heavy traffic in both troops and civilians.

Summer 1963: last steam train departs from KING'S CROSS STATION.

1966: *Flying Scotsman* cuts journey time from KING'S CROSS STATION to Edinburgh to 5 hrs 50 mins.

1978: High Speed Train from KING'S CROSS STATION reaches Edinburgh in 4hrs 50mins.

1983: thieves use smoke bombs to escape with £65,000 from new KING'S CROSS STATION Travel Centre.

1987: East Coast Route from KING'S CROSS STATION electrified as far as Peterborough.

London & North Eastern Railway 4-6-2 locomotive no: 4472 the *Flying Scotsman.*

THE ANGEL ISLINGTON

(N1/London Borough of Islington)

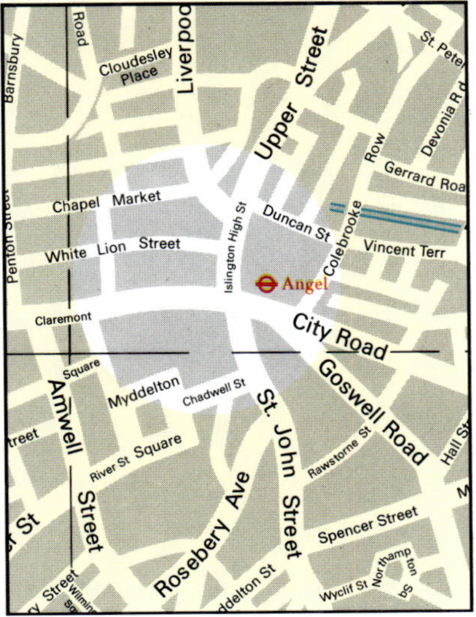

MONOPOLY valuation: £100

Current valuation: £360,000,000

Location description

Just over 1km east of KING'S CROSS STATION, THE ANGEL ISLINGTON – formerly a bustling coaching inn on the Great North Road – was restored as a Co-operative Society bank in 1981-2. Today, the area immediately around it is one of the most famous parts of London and known simply as Angel, with Angel Mews and the Angel tube station flanking the former tavern. Islington, once a tiny, outlying hamlet mentioned in William the Conqueror's Domesday survey, is now an inner London district engulfed by the great metropolis which sprawls a further 15km to its north. It forms a curious blend of working-class terraces, arty town houses and fashionable *pieds-à-terre*.

Derivation of name

The name Islington derives originally from the late Anglo-Saxon 'Gislandune' which meant literally Gisla's Hill. Islington does indeed command one of the highest summits around north London and once enjoyed panoramic views over the metropolis. By the time of *Domesday Book* it was recorded as Isendone and Iseldone, and usage has further corrupted it to the Islington of today.

Many inns have the name 'Angel' and most have the same derivation. Before the reign of Henry VIII it was common for the numerous monasteries to have travellers' guest houses, many of which were called 'Angel of the Salutation'. An illustrated sign (in this case the Angel Gabriel saluting the Virgin Mary) announced the guest house to often illiterate travellers. When

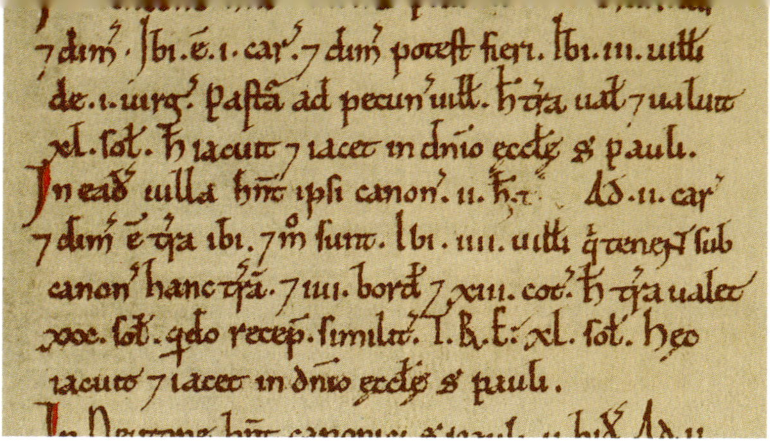

The name 'Isendone' is recorded in the 11thC *Domesday Book* of William the Conqueror.

Henry dissolved the monasteries in the 16thC the guest houses were frequently sold off and maintained commercially as inns, normally still under the same name and sign. In the following century, with the puritanical Cromwellians in power, all reference to the Virgin was obliterated. Any proprietor of an 'Angel of the Salutation' would demote his establishment to mere 'Angel' and discard or redevise the sign that so incautiously depicted the mother of Christ. THE ANGEL ISLINGTON was possibly originally attached to the nearby 12thC Priory of St John of Jerusalem, nothing of which remains today but St John's Gate and the crypt of St John's, Clerkenwell.

Short history

In Gisla's day Islington was probably little more than a small settlement nestling in a clearing of the Great Forest of Middlesex. As the forest's oaken limits receded it developed into a distinct village set in open parkland that by Tudor times gave way to more intensive dairy farming for the supply of milk to the city. For three centuries Londoners were attracted to 'merrie Islington' with its archery butts, taverns and tea gardens. Early in the 15thC causeways were built over the marshes of Moorfields along which Londoners could walk to the slopes of Islington. The Elizabethans went there to shoot wildfowl and the Georgians took the waters there from wells in elegant garden settings, frequently visited by royalty.

By the early 19thC Islington was taking London's growing overflow with the construction of regular terraces and broad plazas. Eventually its attractiveness diminished as it became a dormitory district for lower-paid workers, a trend reversed in recent years by the conversion of some workers' terraces into desirable bijou town-houses. This rejuvenation is making Islington one of the more fashionable parts of north London.

The Angel itself was for many centuries the nearest staging post to London where north- and south-bound coaches could change horses. Standing opposite a clump of elm trees, this large inn occupied a strategic position at the head of the busy routes entering both the City (Goswell Road) and London's largest meat market at Smithfield (St John Street). Nearby were enclosures for cattle being driven to Smithfield. At night, when the surrounding countryside was infested with thugs and footpads, travellers found the Angel particularly convenient. One legendary highwayman, the gentlemanly Claude Duval (euphemistically said to 'dance a gavot' with his female victims), frequently operated this route. In fact, so hazardous were the roads that it was common for nocturnal travellers to be escorted by

Innkeepers frequently had a financial interest in the coaches and horses that brought them their trade. One former 19thC owner, William Chaplin, owned a chain of London inns, sixty coaching lines and nearly 2,000 horses. At the height of the coaching era more than 1,500 coaches started and ended their journeys in London. In 1819 the Angel Inn was completely rebuilt as a hotel, and again in 1899 when it became a Lyons' Corner House. It closed in 1960 and remained derelict for twenty years.

Islington itself has always been a home to radicals and reformers. Its history is peppered with names that have reorientated human thought. Radicals as diverse as John Wesley and Vladimir Ilyich Lenin, Edward Irving and Edmund Halley – all have had associations with Gisla's Hill. Even today many intellectuals and free thinkers are proud to live in a village of London that justly values its historic significance and independence.

The old Angel Inn as it was in 1808, eleven years before its reconstruction as a hotel.

Points of interest

Sadler's Wells Theatre (Rosebery Avenue), birthplace of English ballet, is the base for the famous Sadler's Wells Royal Ballet company. Thomas Sadler, enterprising owner of a pleasure-garden with a medicinal well where visitors could drink much more than water, opened his 'musick house' as a side-attraction in 1683.

Camden Passage Antique Market Since the 1960s this picturesque market has become noted for its antique and bric-à-brac shops and stalls, attracting interest from all over the world. Camden Passage's Italian and French restaurants are among the best in London.

The Business Design Centre.

Chapel Street Market is one of largest of London's traditional street markets. Its stalls of seasonal fruit and vegetables, meats and wet fish, clothes and children's toys are surrounded by bustling pavement cafés and friendly pubs.

The **Royal Agricultural Hall** (Upper Street) Built in 1861 for the Smithfield Society, this graceful Crystal Palace-style structure covering 1.2ha is still known popularly as the 'Aggie'. The World's Fair was held here from 1873. The famous Crufts Dog Show started here in 1891. It saw cattle shows, circuses, exhibitions – even, in 1870, Britain's first and last Spanish bullfight, in a ring suddenly thick with RSPCA officials. Today the Aggie has been imaginatively restored and developed as the **Business Design Centre** complete with display areas, offices, restaurants and bars.

Collins Music Hall Here at the north end of Islington Green celebrated artistes like Marie Lloyd, Charlie Chaplin, Gracie Fields, Max Miller and Tommy Trinder performed. Built in 1862, this famous theatre was razed by fire in 1958.

Famous people

Sir Walter Raleigh (1552–1618), soldier, sailor and author who so dazzled Queen Elizabeth I, lived in a hostelry in Upper Street. In the ancient Old Queen's Head tavern (Essex Road) he supposedly introduced his friends to the pleasures of tobacco.

Alexander Cruden (1701–70), harebrained tutor, bookseller and author of the classic *Concordance of the Holy Scriptures,* lodged in Camden Passage where he died at his prayers.

Thomas Lord (1755–1832), a name perpetuated by the famous Lords cricket ground in St John's Wood, founded his cricket club in 1782 in pleasure gardens near Chapel Market.

Thomas Paine (1737–1809), English radical on whose *Rights of Man* the United States Constitution was based, lived at the Angel. The first part of this persuasive work was written here, almost certainly in the Angel Inn itself.

Charles Lamb (1775–1834), brilliant writer and essayist, lived in Duncan Terrace with his insane sister Mary to whom he devoted his unhappy life. From a foreign fellow-clerk in his office Lamb took his pseudonym 'Elia': from this *nom de plume* nearby Elia Street in turn took its name.

Vladimir Ilyich Lenin (1870–1924), who edited the revolutionary journal *Iskra* ('The Spark') in Islington, and **Leon Trotsky** (1879–1940), radical Russian émigré journalist, frequently met at the Crown and Woolpack (St John Street) to plot the downfall of the Czar. After Lenin, Trotsky was to become the second most powerful man in Russia.

Joe Orton (1933–67), prominent 20thC playwright, lived near the Angel in Noel Road. His stylish black comedies featuring corruption, violence and sexual perversion included *Entertaining Mr Sloane, Loot* and *What the Butler Saw.*

CHANCE

ADVANCE TO TRAFALGAR SQUARE
IF YOU PASS "GO" COLLECT £200

What is the overall height of Nelson's Column in TRAFALGAR SQUARE?
a) 22.7m
b) 56.3m
c) 145m

SPEEDING FINE £15

On which of the following MONOPOLY spaces might you conceivably exceed the speed limit?
a) LEICESTER SQUARE
b) PARK LANE
c) VINE STREET

YOUR BUILDING LOAN MATURES RECEIVE £150

At which address is the London office of the world's largest building society?
a) PALL MALL
b) OXFORD STREET
c) STRAND

GO TO JAIL
MOVE DIRECTLY TO JAIL
DO NOT PASS "GO" DO NOT COLLECT £200

In which of the following prisons was the crank invented to 'grind the wind'?
a) The Tower of London
b) Fleet Prison
c) Pentonville Prison

ADVANCE TO PALL MALL
IF YOU PASS "GO" COLLECT £200

Which of the following sports bears the most striking similarities to pall-mall?
a) squash
b) croquet
c) cricket

answers: bbccb

EUSTON ROAD

(NW1/London Borough of Camden)

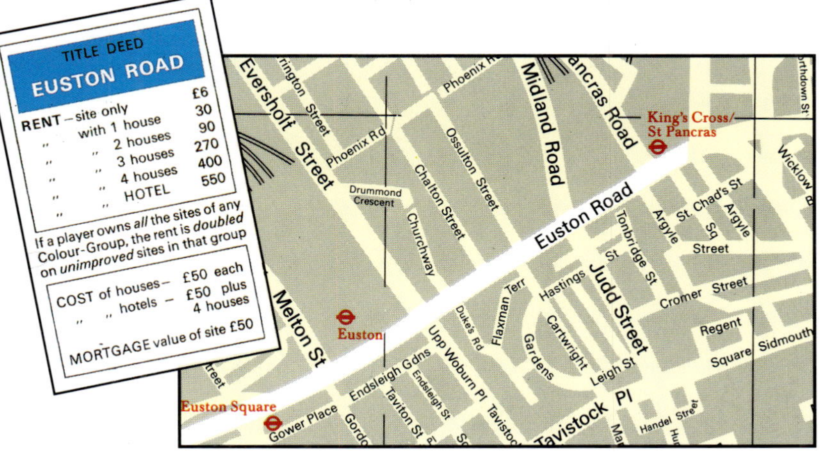

MONOPOLY valuation: £100
Current valuation: £165,900,000

Location description

A major arterial route running approximately east-west from KING'S CROSS STATION to Regent's Park, EUSTON ROAD is a busy commercial thoroughfare 1.75km in length. Along its northern side lie three of London's most important main-line railway stations.

Derivation of name

The landlords of the ground over which the present EUSTON ROAD passes were the Fitzroys, Dukes of Grafton and Earls of Euston. A small village just south of Thetford in Suffolk, Euston originally meant 'Eof's estate'. It was in memory of the Duke of Grafton's son, Lord Euston, that the road was renamed in 1857.

Short history

EUSTON ROAD forms a 1.75km section of London's first ring road or northern bypass. The New Road, as it was known, skirted the then northern edge of London, running from Paddington to Islington. It was built from 1756 by the 2nd Duke of Grafton to avoid Oxford Street and Holborn when driving fat cattle from his estates in the west to the huge Smithfield Market just outside the City. Its creation was sanctioned despite strenuous petitions made to the House of Commons by the Capper family. The Cappers, who lived in the Long Fields on the south of the proposed route, vainly argued that the dust clouds raised by the driven cattle would ruin their hay.

When first constructed London's first bypass ran through open countryside.

Just to its north sprang up London's railway termini for passengers to and from the North and Midlands: MARYLEBONE STATION, Euston Station, St Pancras Station and KING'S CROSS STATION – like four caged and crouching lions eager but forbidden to leap this impudent barrier.

Even the route of the first underground railway was governed by the New Road. In 1854 the Metropolitan Railway Company secured permission for a 'cut-and-cover' line along the route of the New Road. It opened in 1863, linking the northern termini with the City and carrying 30,000 passengers on its first day.

Points of interest

Euston Station Midway along EUSTON ROAD on its northern edge, Euston Station was the first of London's main line termini to be built, although the present structure is not the original having been substantially rebuilt and enlarged in the 1960s. Built for the London and Birmingham Railway, the original station opened in July 1837. From it, for the first year, six trains ran daily to Harrow, Watford and Boxmoor. Then on 17 September 1838 the first train journey from London to Birmingham was accomplished, the 112 miles being covered in just over five hours. In 1968 Queen Elizabeth II opened a new Euston Station, most of the original having been dismantled in the face of robust opposition.

Right: Charles Fitzroy, 2nd Duke of Grafton, initiator of London's first bypass.

George Gilbert Scott's phantastic 1872 façade to St Pancras Station retains its air of Gothic romance.

St Pancras Station In 1868 the Midland Railway proudly opened their new London terminus in EUSTON ROAD. Although neither the first nor the largest, it was nevertheless a remarkable triumph of Victorian engineering. Its glass and iron train shed was 210 metres in length. Each of its 56-tonne ribs spans 73 metres and is 30 metres above the rails at its apex.

In 1868-72 the 250-bed **Midland Grand Hotel** was added, enclosing the train shed and forming a façade to EUSTON ROAD. Planned by George Gilbert Scott, its romantic Gothic style of pinnacles, towers and gables reflected the spirit of his earlier but rejected design for government offices in WHITEHALL. In fact, Scott was later to write: 'It is often spoken of to me as the finest building in London; my own belief is that it is possibly too good for its purpose, but having been disappointed through Lord Palmerston of my ardent hope of carrying out my style in the Government Offices . . . I was glad to be able to erect one building in that style in London.' It was once described as the best conducted hotel in the Empire. Converted for office use in 1935 under the name of St Pancras Chambers, plans were proposed in the 1980s to restore this Victorian fantasy to its former 'purpose' as a hotel.

KING'S CROSS STATION, completed in 1852 at the eastern end of EUSTON ROAD, was probably the most handsome of all London's railway stations. When it opened as the terminus of the Great Northern Railway it was the largest station in England and was shared by the Midland Railway until St Pancras opened.

Wellcome Institute for the History of Medicine (#183) Sir Henry Wellcome, the manufacturing chemist, accumulated an exceptional library dedicated to medicine. Housed here, it now contains over 400,000 books, 100,000 letters, 100,000 prints and drawings, 38,000 photographic images, 14,000 manuscripts and 900 oil paintings.

Above: John Fitzgerald Kennedy (1917-63).
Right: British Telecom's communication tower commands views along the entire length of EUSTON ROAD.

John F Kennedy Just as EUSTON ROAD becomes Marylebone Road there stands an impressive bronze bust of this 34th United States President. Donated by readers of the *Sunday Times*, it was unveiled in 1965 by the President's brothers Robert and Edward.

British Telecom Tower (Howland Street) This former Post Office Tower just off EUSTON ROAD was erected in 1964, ensuring interference-free telecommunications and satellite transmissions. At 189m (including its 12m radar mast) this is one of the tallest structures in London and was originally equipped with a revolving restaurant and observation platform.

The **British Library** (Great Russell Street), one of the most important in the world, is scheduled to move in 1991 to new purpose-built premises in EUSTON ROAD. With a statutory duty to preserve every publication in the United Kingdom, the library houses over 16 million volumes, requiring 13km of new shelving annually.

Famous people

Dukes of Grafton The 1st Duke of Grafton was originally plain Henry Fitzroy, the son of Charles II by one of his mistresses, Barbara Villiers. Henry was married at the age of nine to Isabella Bennet, the five-year-old only daughter of Lord Arlington who left her a country estate at Euston as well as the Manor of Tottenham Court. From the estate in Suffolk Henry derived the title Earl of Euston (he was later also created Duke of Grafton) and from the manor he derived much of his land in London. It was Henry's son, Charles Fitzroy, 2nd Duke of Grafton, who built the New (Euston) Road.

The Capper family Capper Street just south of EUSTON ROAD in WC1 was named after the Capper family who so vigorously opposed the construction of the New Road. The Capper sisters were described by an official of the British Museum: 'They wore riding habits and men's hats. One used to ride after boys flying kites with a large pair of shears to cut the strings. The other seized the clothes of those who trespassed to bathe.'

George Shillibeer (1797-1866), Bloomsbury coach-builder, introduced buses to London in 1829. His first three-horse omnibus, 'running upon the Parisian mode', travelled in 1829 along the New Road from Paddington to Bank for a fare of 1s 6d. Almost ruined by the fierce competition that sprang up, the pioneering Shillibeer eventually converted his omnibuses into hearses.

George Shillibeer's omnibus, seating up to twenty passengers, was modelled on the buses of Paris.

Popular associations: Pentonville Prison

PENTONVILLE ROAD

(N1/London Borough of Islington)

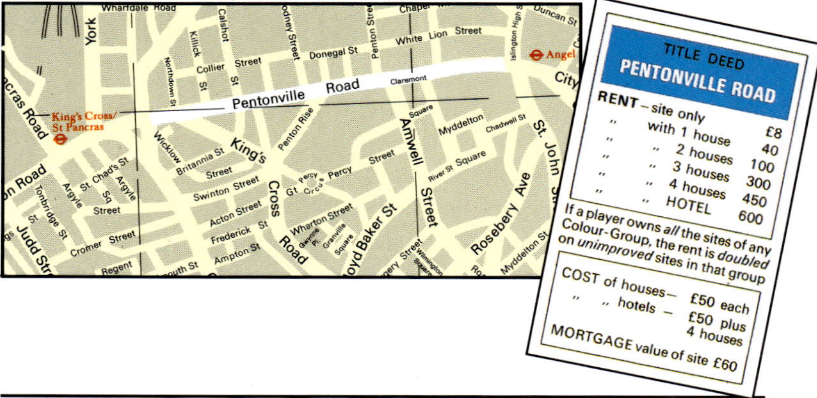

MONOPOLY valuation: £120
Current valuation: £61,950,000

Location description

The final section of London's first northern bypass, the New Road of 1756, PENTONVILLE ROAD links THE ANGEL ISLINGTON with KING'S CROSS STATION and EUSTON ROAD. This is the most northerly of all the MONOPOLY streets, a busy medley of hotels, commercial offices, automotive workshops and imaginative housing schemes.

Derivation of name

The name of Pentonville is taken from Henry Penton, MP for Winchester, on whose rural estate on Islington Hill a planned suburb was laid out in the 1770s. The use of the French *-ville* to describe newly developed areas was very much in vogue by the late 18thC. Several adjoining streets such as Penton Rise and Penton Street also recall the name of Henry Penton.

Short history

Following on from EUSTON ROAD, PENTONVILLE ROAD forms the last stretch of the original New Road of 1756, a peripheral link between the residential areas in the west and the City in the east. In 1761 it was continued eastwards from the Angel as the City Road. In its early days it was a rural highway so beset by footpads and other outlaws that at night mounted patrols would escort theatre-goers home from Sadler's Wells.

After the establishment in 1855 of the Metropolitan Board of Works, the capital's first overall local authority, the streets of central London were extensively renamed. The explosive development of the metropolis had resulted in dozens of streets with identical names: 'King Streets', 'Union Streets', 'New Streets', 'New Roads' – all added to the confusion and all were doomed to redesignation. Thus it was that the eastern section of this New Road, skirting as it did the burgeoning suburb of Pentonville, was restyled PENTONVILLE ROAD in 1857.

Above: Looking westwards towards the sunset and EUSTON ROAD, this 1884 oil by John O'Connor captures the mood of 19thC PENTONVILLE ROAD. St Pancras Station is clearly visible, dwarfing the clock tower of neighbouring KING'S CROSS STATION.
Right: A similar view, one hundred years later.

Convicts exercising at Pentonville Prison in 1862. As a model prison built on the separate system, communication between prisoners was restricted – hence the masks.

Points of interest

Pentonville Prison Although probably associated in the minds of most with PENTONVILLE ROAD, Pentonville Prison is actually in Caledonian Road, just to the north. Built in 1840, it was here that Roger Casement was hanged for high treason in 1916. Almost one hundred years had elapsed since the previous hanging for treason in England – the execution of the Cato Street Conspirators in 1820. Planned by Sir Joshua Jebb, Pentonville Prison was modelled on the radial pattern of Haviland's Eastern Penitentiary in Philadelphia, USA. It was the first of its kind in England and reminded at least one Victorian correspondent of 'the Crystal Palace stripped of all its contents'. The crank, a Victorian hard-labour contraption designed to 'grind the wind', was invented at Pentonville Prison.

The London Hydraulic Power Company PENTONVILLE ROAD, along with EUSTON ROAD, marks the northern limits of the vast network of subterranean water pipes that provided a potent source of power for London's Victorian industry. Through these pipes was pumped untreated water at a pressure of 1000kg/cm^2, delivering the power to operate lifting gear and cranes, production presses, lifts, even safety curtains in West End theatres. The great pressure was generated at five pumping stations around London. The London Hydraulic Power Company, founded in 1871, was allowed by statute to extract over 100 million litres of water per week. Today, its waterless cast-iron pipes are still valuable, forming superb conduits for the spaghetti-maze of telephone and television cables that criss-cross modern London.

London Female Penitentiary (#166) In this converted mansion 19thC 'fallen women' were rehabilitated. Up to 100 contrite and remorseful inmates could be accommodated at any one time.

The Medici Society (#34/42), who pioneered high quality reproduction of great paintings by the collotype process, have their head office in PENTONVILLE ROAD. Founded in 1908 by Philip Lee Warner, the name Medici was chosen in memory of the great Florentine family of the Italian Renaissance.

Famous people

Joseph Grimaldi (1779–1837), the tragi-comic clown of Italian parentage, was a regular performer before fashionable audiences at nearby Sadler's Wells. Commemorated here in Joseph Grimaldi Park (corner of Rodney Street), he lies buried in the graveyard of the now redundant church of St James, PENTONVILLE ROAD. Here also lie **Aaron Hurst**, architect of the church, and **Henry Penton**, developer of Pentonville.

Sir Roger David Casement (1864-1916), British public official and Irish nationalist who liaised with Germany during the First World War, was arrested in 1916, convicted of high treason at the Old Bailey and hanged at Pentonville Prison on 3 August. The Irish authorities later gave him a state funeral.

Lenin – formerly **Ilyanov** – (1870-1924). At the top of Vernon Rise, just off Penton Rise, a plaque marks the London domicile of this prominent Russian revolutionary in exile, stating simply: 'Vladimir Ilyich Ilyanov, founder of the USSR'. Lenin was destined to become the first leader of Soviet Russia. Today, queues of Russians file endlessly past his preserved body at the mausoleum in Red Square, Moscow.

'Mr Grimaldi as Clown.'

COMMUNITY CHEST
COMMUNITY CHEST
MARYLEBONE STATION BRITISH RAILWAYS £200
MARYLEBONE STATION BRITISH RAILWAYS £200
BOW STREET £180
BOW STREET £180
COMMUNITY CHEST
MARLBOROUGH STREET £180
MARLBOROUGH STREET £180
VINE STREET £200
VINE STREET £200
STRAND £220
STRAND £220
FREE
500 MONOPOLY 500
100 MONOPOLY 100
50 MONOPOLY 50
TITLE DEED
TITLE DEED
TITLE DEED
TITLE DEED
TITLE DEED
TITLE DEED PICCADILLY
RENT – site only £22
" with 1 house 120
" " 2 houses 360
" " 3 houses 850
" " 4 houses 1025
" " HOTEL 1200
If a player owns all the sites of any Colour-Group, the rent is doubled on unimproved sites in that group
COST of houses – £150 each
WATER WORKS

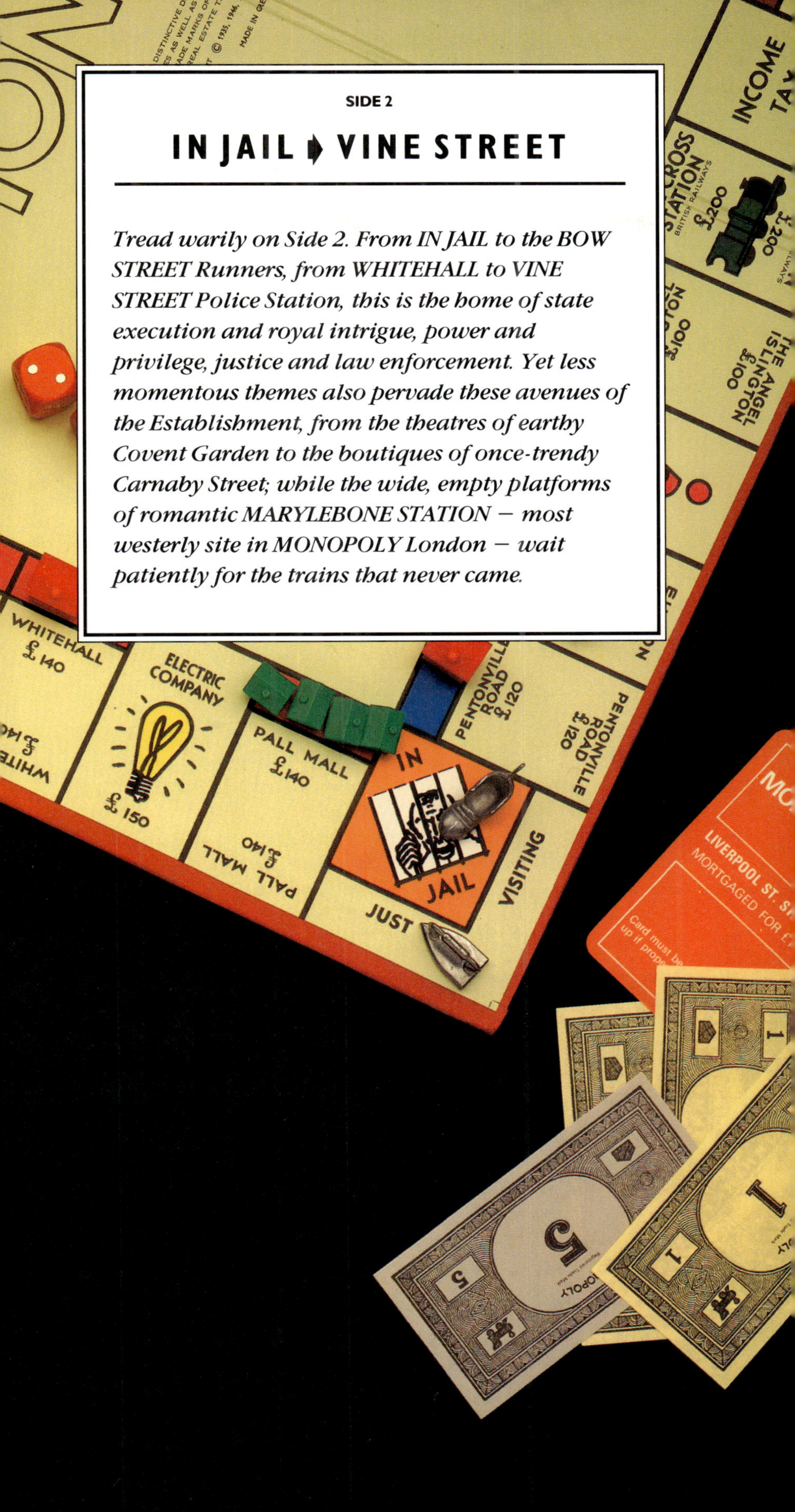

SIDE 2

IN JAIL ➧ VINE STREET

Tread warily on Side 2. From IN JAIL to the BOW STREET Runners, from WHITEHALL to VINE STREET Police Station, this is the home of state execution and royal intrigue, power and privilege, justice and law enforcement. Yet less momentous themes also pervade these avenues of the Establishment, from the theatres of earthy Covent Garden to the boutiques of once-trendy Carnaby Street; while the wide, empty platforms of romantic MARYLEBONE STATION – most westerly site in MONOPOLY London – wait patiently for the trains that never came.

IN JAIL

The Tower of London

'So the heart be right,
it no matter which way the head lies.'

Sir Walter Raleigh (1552–1618)

After William of Normandy conquered Britain in 1066 he constructed a series of fortresses alongside the walls of London. To the west were Montfichet's Tower and Baynard's Castle, both long demolished: to the east his famous Tower of London, firmly founded on Roman fortifications even then nearly a thousand years old. Situated on the banks of the Thames, it naturally controlled the river approaches to London. When completed in 1097, the Tower represented the ultimate in 11thC European technology – a large and sophisticated stronghold 'fixed with a mortar tempered by the blood of animals' and built to specifications unknown to the British.

Today the Tower of London, much enlarged, is unquestionably one of the premier landmarks in the world. Massive and forbidding, this awesome fortress sprawls across some seven moated hectares. During its long and gruesome history it has served as citadel, palace, garrison, arsenal, treasury, mint, observatory and – above all – state prison and scene of execution. Peasant and prince, saint and sinner – all were IN JAIL here and many have perished here.

With this moving reconstruction, the Victorian painter John Millais helped to perpetuate the tragic romance of the 'Princes in the Tower'.

Famous prisoners

The twelve-year old **Edward V** (1470–83) and his younger brother the **Duke of York** – the 'Princes in the Tower' – were murdered (probably smothered) in the Bloody Tower where they had been incarcerated by their power-hungry uncle, Richard Duke of Gloucester – shortly to be crowned Richard III. Despite intense speculation, Richard's complicity in their deaths – long suspected – has never been conclusively proven, but recent forensic evidence is increasingly damning.

Left: One thousand years separate the Tower of London and adjacent Tower Bridge, but both are among the premier landmarks of the modern world. In the background is London Bridge, built near the site of the original Roman crossing.

Sir Thomas More (1478–1535), philosopher, saint and statesman, was imprisoned in the Bell Tower after refusing to take the Oath of Supremacy. He died 'the King's good servant but God's first', staying the executioner's axe briefly to clear his long grey beard – 'for this has committed no treason.'

Anne Boleyn (c1504–36), second wife of Henry VIII, lived out her last days here. Condemned to death for adultery, she walked calmly out to her noon-day execution, observing to her guard: 'I have a little neck.' It was severed cleanly by the Calais sword that she had requested in place of the customary axe. Within six years Henry's fifth wife, **Catherine Howard** (c1520–42), was also brought here by river through the ominous Traitor's Gate, passing *en route* the heads of her lovers Culpepper and Dereham exhibited on London Bridge. Beheaded on the axeman's block, she declared defiantly: 'I die a queen, but I would rather have died the wife of Culpepper.'

Lady Jane Grey (1537–54), hapless, uncrowned Queen of England, spent her nine-day reign in the Tower of London. Having watched one bitter, winter morning as the headless body of her husband was trundled back from execution outside, sixteen-year old Lady Jane was beheaded later that day on the more secluded and decorous Tower Green just inside the perimeter walls.

The Union flag flies over the White Tower.

Few prisoners who entered through Traitor's Gate re-emerged alive; yet this watergate was also used by the royal barge and for provisions.

Guy Fawkes (1570–1606) and his co-conspirators were imprisoned and barbarously tortured in the Tower following their abortive 1605 Gunpowder Plot to blow up the Houses of Parliament and Scottish-born king. Interrogation in the Queen's House revealed that one of Guy Fawkes's goals had been 'to blow Scotsmen back into Scotland'.

Simon Fraser, Lord Lovat (c1667–1747), Scottish chief and Jacobite agent, was executed on Tower Hill just outside the Tower's perimeter. Lovat distinguished himself by being the last person in Britain to be beheaded officially – taking with him twelve spectators crushed to death by the collapse of a stand.

In the First and Second World Wars many spies were executed by firing squad near the Martin Tower; and **Rudolf Hess** (1894-1987), Deputy Führer of Nazi Germany sentenced to life-imprisonment after the War, spent four days captive here following his fruitless secret mission to Britain in May 1941.

PALL MALL

(SW1/City of Westminster)

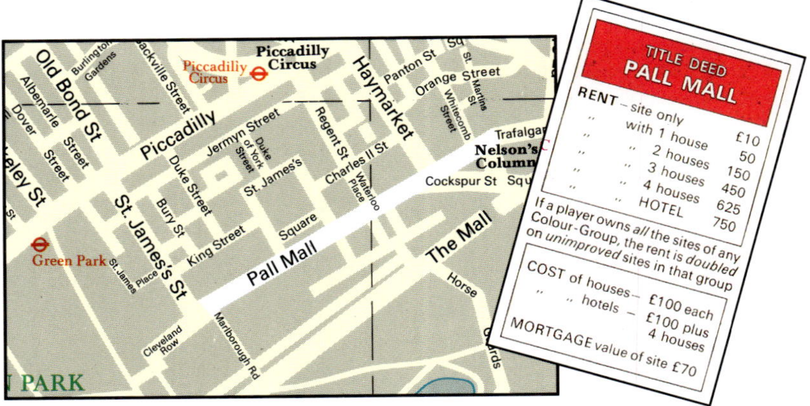

MONOPOLY valuation: £140
Current valuation: £264,000,000

Location description

'If one must have a villa in summer to dwell,
Oh, give me the sweet shady side of PALL MALL!'

Charles Morris (1745-1838)

Extending from St James's Palace in the west to Haymarket in the east, PALL MALL (also pronounced 'pel mel') has a royal and aristocratic lineage. Traversing the district of St James's, PALL MALL is celebrated primarily for its prestigious gentlemen's clubs, where the wealthy and noble are assured of the discreetest comforts. Today it is still a broad, elegant avenue of classical buildings, but the former stately residences and many of the clubs have been replaced by expensive offices and the occasional specialist shop.

Derivation of name

The name is taken from a fashionable 16thC and 17thC ball game, something of a hybrid between croquet and golf, in which a boxwood ball was driven through a suspended iron ring at the end of an alley. Imported from France (*palle-maille*) and originating in Italy (*pallo a maglio* = ball to mallet), pall-mall was a 'gentleman-like sport' played in the highest echelons of society. PALL MALL occupies the site of a former pall-mall alley.

Short history

The development of PALL MALL, and the whole of St James's, stemmed from the proximity of the royal court. The Palace of St James's was built as a hunting lodge for Henry VIII. Many royal children were born here; and a condemned Charles I spent his last night here. But it became the sovereign's principal home only in 1698 when WHITEHALL Palace was gutted by fire. It remains the official court. Even now, when the chief residence is

Left: St James's Palace, *raison d'être* for PALL MALL and the district of St James's, matchlessly preserves the architecture of Tudor London.
Below: Charles II was born at St James's Palace in 1630.

Buckingham Palace, it is to the Court of St James's that foreign ambassadors are accredited.

Pall-mall was one of the games that Charles II played with his mistresses in the park at St James's Palace. But the royal pall-mall alley was so often obscured by traffic dust that a new road was laid out in 1661 along an older pall-mall alley just to the north. The new thoroughfare was officially designated Catherine Street; but the memory of its former use survived the queen, Catherine of Braganza, and its popular name of PALL MALL prevailed over official usage.

PALL MALL was soon a fashionable, highly desirable address. Fine homes were built for the aristocracy and others who had important business at Court. By the early 1700s expensive shops served the grand new houses as well as the palace. By the mid-1700s it had attracted the attention of writers and artists and became famous for its bachelor lodgings.

Amid the great abodes, the fabulous gardens, the expensive clockmakers and the specialist booksellers were humbler businesses – the coffee and chocolate houses from which evolved the clubs of St James's. The coffee house was rendezvous to aristocratic and intellectual London society. It was the centre for news, gossip and free discussion. From the like-minded clientèle who met regularly the first clubs emerged: there were discreet gambling clubs; lofty political clubs; comradely servicemen's clubs; learned writers' clubs; Bohemian artists' clubs; even lively sporting clubs. But it was generally not until the 19thC that imposing private club premises were built. Today nothing so vulgar as a brass plate announces a PALL MALL club – refuge of the élite, haunt of the privileged, preserve of men.

Looking eastwards along PALL MALL in 1832: on the extreme right is the Carlton Club; beyond it are the Reform, the Travellers', the Atheneum and the United Service. In the distance the Duke of York surmounts his column. Permanent street lighting by gas has already been installed.

Despite considerable rebuilding and redevelopment, by the early 1800s PALL MALL still boasted some magnificent private mansions ('fit for the residence of the wealthy and noble') like Buckingham House, Marlborough House, York House and Carlton House.

It was at Carlton House that the world first witnessed the magical illumination of an entire street by gas. Here FA Winsor, a resourceful Moravian, celebrated the 1805 birthday of the Prince of Wales with a public display of gas lights. PALL MALL itself had to wait until 1820 for its permanent installation. Ten years later the flamboyant Winsor died poverty-stricken in Paris; and in Kensal Green Cemetery a monument recalls his achievement: 'At evening time it shall be light' *(Zachariah* 14v7*)*.

PALL MALL

Points of interest

Temple of Health and Hymen Schomberg House was once base to an eccentric Scottish charlatan, Dr James Graham. In 1881 he opened his famous temple in Pall Mall. It was well equipped. There was the amazing 'Medico-Electrical Apparatus'; and miraculous mud baths in which pulchritudinous young ladies wallowed nude, convincing the gullible of their efficacy. Then there was Dr Graham's mirror-lined 'Grand Celestial Bed', serenading its occupants with music. In it his wealthy patrons were so 'powerfully agitated in the delights of love' that 'even the barren' would conceive perfect progeny. The fee of £100 per night included the 'celebrated lecture on Generation' delivered from the 'Celestial Throne' by Dr Graham himself.

Schomberg House (#80/82) was reconstructed in 1957 behind its original exterior.

Hell Corner During the 19thC the east end of PALL MALL was worked extensively by prostitutes – those not servicing the royal court at the west end. Shop girls, servants, hatters, fishwives – women of all trades supplemented their wages in this way. In fact more prostitutes operated in and around Haymarket, dubbed Hell Corner, than anywhere else in London.

Freemasons' Arms (#32 Downshire Hill, NW3). In this heathside public house in Hampstead, may be seen the last remaining pall-mall court in England.

The clubs Many clubs that originated in PALL MALL have since moved to other addresses or ceased to exist. Some of the existing clubs were founded elsewhere. The Athenaeum (#107) Past and present membership of this the most intellectually élite of all London clubs includes prime ministers and archbishops. The Athenaeum in Rome was a university founded by the Emperor Hadrian. The Travellers' Club (#106), founded in 1819 for those returning from abroad, is now purely a social club. The Reform Club (#104/5) In its smoking room Phineas Fogg accepted the challenge to circumnavigate the globe in 80 days. The Royal Automobile Club (#89) In its dining room the spies Burgess and Maclean lunched calmly before fleeing the country. Club amenities include a rifle range, post office, swimming pool and Turkish baths. The United Oxford and Cambridge University Club (#71/77) Membership is limited exclusively to members of the universities of Cambridge and Oxford. The Junior Carlton (#30), formed in 1864, relieved the lengthy waiting list for the Carlton Club. The Army and Navy Club (#36/39) is affectionately known as 'the Rag', an allusion by one of its early members to the former Rag and Famish brothel in Cranbourne Street.

The Institute of Directors, the world's largest organisation to represent individual business leaders, occupies the former home of the United Service Club at #116.

Star and Garter Reputed to dispense 'the best claret in England', the Star and Garter was an exclusive 18thC PALL MALL tavern. Many clubs met or were formed here. At one meeting Lord Byron fatally wounded his cousin in a sword fight. In the ensuing murder trial Byron was acquitted. The smart *Je ne sais quoi* Club also met here, often attended by the Prince of Wales, later George IV.

Nell Gwynne, aged about twenty in this portrait, had at least one son by Charles II, probably two (Simon Verelst c1670).

Famous people

Nell Gwynne (c1650-87), one of Charles II's mistresses, lived at #79 Pall Mall. With the sole exception of this site all the south side of Pall Mall is Crown property. The freehold to #79 was transferred from the Crown in 1676 when the effervescent orange seller, furious that her royal lover was offering her a leasehold, insisted passionately that she 'had always conveyed free under the Crown' and refused to live in a house that she did not entirely own.

Site of Nell Gwynne's house at #79.

The Duke of York (1763-1827)

'The noble Duke of York,
He had ten thousand men,
He marched them up to the top of the hill,
And he marched them down again.'

Anon. – first printed 1913

At the east end of PALL MALL, in Waterloo Place, a statue of the Duke of York (Queen Victoria's wicked uncle and second son of George III) surmounts a very tall, well proportioned column – out of his creditors' reach according to his detractors. At the west end of PALL MALL stands the lavish edifice that ran up so many of his debts – originally York, then Stafford, now Lancaster House. On the duke's death, it was sold to the Marquess of Stafford by the government who discharged the debts. The marquess himself became a duke; and his duchess became one of Queen Victoria's closest friends. The queen once commented on visiting the duchess 'I have come from my house to your palace.'

ELECTRIC COMPANY

MONOPOLY valuation: £150
Current valuation: £1,000,000,000

Electricity illuminates the Christmas lights of REGENT STREET and dapples the silver screens of LEICESTER SQUARE. This enigmatic force elevates the plush lifts of PARK LANE and once powered the toiling presses in FLEET STREET. It warms the cosy clubs of PALL MALL, pulls the express trains of KING'S CROSS STATION and cools the humming computers in WHITEHALL.

Yet electricity was virtually unknown in London before the 1870s when it was first introduced for lighting. By the 1890s it was powering London's underground trains and within twenty more years seventy different power stations were generating a dizzying assortment of voltages for the capital.

Today, the production and distribution of electricity has been rationalised. Manufactured by the Central Electricity Generating Board, it is purchased in bulk by MONOPOLY London's ELECTRIC COMPANY, the London Electricity Board, who deliver and retail it through subterranean cables across an urban area of some 700km^2 with a total population of 5,000,000.

All told, the London Electricity Board's 7,000 staff annually supply 2,000,000 customers – who together consume over 16,000,000,000kWh of electricity at a cost of £900,000,000, demanding during the winter months a simultaneous maximum supply peaking at 4,000,000kWh.

With a capacity to generate over 500 megawatts of electricity, Battersea Power Station consumed some 10,000 tonnes of coal weekly and supplied almost one-fifth of London's total electricity supplies. After fifty years of service, it was sold in the mid-1980s for conversion into a massive Thames-side leisure complex.

WHITEHALL

(SW1/City of Westminster)

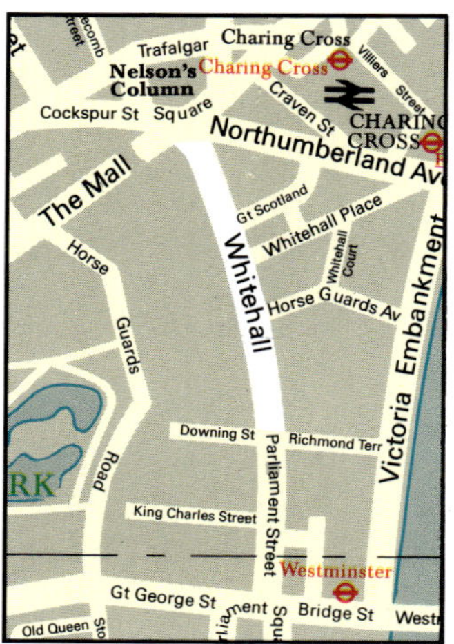

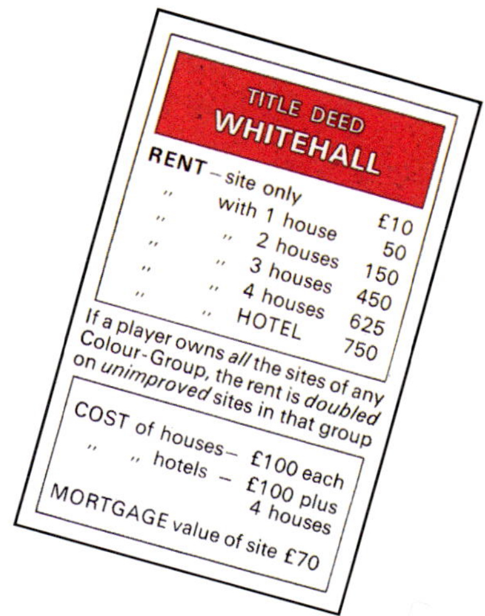

MONOPOLY valuation: £140

Current valuation: £840,000,000

Location description

'You must no more call it York Place, that's past:
For since the Cardinal fell, that title's lost;
'Tis now the King's and called WHITEHALL.'

Shakespeare *Henry VIII*

A broad avenue of 600m curving due south from TRAFALGAR SQUARE towards the Houses of Parliament and Westminster Abbey, WHITEHALL is without doubt the most majestic street on the MONOPOLY board. The imposing government offices that line its flanks today are the source of its notorious synonymity with red tape and bureaucracy. Home of a myriad civil servants, whose deskbound drudgery once administered an empire, it is nevertheless an exhilarating site with an indefinable air of power, plot and pageant.

Derivation of name

WHITEHALL as a centre of government administration owes its existence and name to the former Royal Palace of WHITEHALL which once sprawled across much of this area. The palace itself acquired its name either from the light hue of its stonework or from the old practice of naming any festive building a 'White Hall'. Whatever the case, the name of WHITEHALL has entered common usage and is defined by the *Concise Oxford Dictionary* simply as: 'British Government; its offices or policy'.

Short history

In the 13thC the property north of Westminster Abbey was sold by its monks to Walter de Gray, Archbishop of York, who donated it to the see of York. For the next 300 years its main dwelling hall, renamed York Place, became the official London residence of all Archbishops of York, conveniently close to the royal Palace of Westminster for their official visits to the capital. In 1514 Cardinal Wolsey became Archbishop of York, lavishly extending York Place, acquiring much adjoining land and adding the Great Hall in 1528, the year before his demise. Here he grandly entertained Henry VIII and his court. The king clearly enjoyed the primate's hospitality, for when Wolsey fell from favour in 1529 he appropriated York Place to himself.

Henry's own court and official residence, the Palace of Westminster, by now more than 500 years old, was decaying. York Place would make a more agreeable and convenient residence. Accordingly he set about enlarging and improving his new acquisition, adding land and buildings to it until it sprawled from the Thames to St James's Park, from Charing Cross to Westminster. The new palace was now called WHITEHALL. No visitor could fail to be impressed by its splendour. Gold was everywhere, from the ceilings and tapestries to the very apparel of the king. To the east, white

Mid-17thC view of WHITEHALL looking south with the Banqueting Hall to the east.

Two symbols of endurance: in naval overcoat a bronze Sir Winston Churchill by Ivor Roberts-Jones looks towards the giant hands of Big Ben.

swans and colourful Thames barges floated gracefully by: to the west, deer ranged effortlessly in royal parkland while lance-bearing knights charged across the expansive new tilt yard. And north-south, through the centre of all this magnificence, ran the broad public thoroughfare that had linked Charing Cross to Westminster since medieval days. Much of this too was now known as WHITEHALL. Across it stood two massive stone gateways, WHITEHALL Gate and King Street Gate, effectively bridges linking the palace property either side of the street. Today, following the fire of 1698 that ensured the transition of the royal court from WHITEHALL to St James's Palace, the only surviving building is Inigo Jones's magnificent stone Banqueting House.

Points of interest

Cabinet War Rooms (Clive Steps, King Charles Street) In 1936 Churchill and others instigated the construction of reinforced basements for the conduct of a war that they perceived as inevitable. By the end of the Second World War this subterranean complex of basements and sub-basements, bombproofed by a vast slab of concrete above, had grown to more than 1ha in area and could accommodate over five hundred persons. Here in the soundproofed Cabinet Room the War Cabinet could meet during air-raids; in the Map Room the Chiefs of Staff would survey Allied and Axis movements on every front; from the Transatlantic Telephone Room the Prime Minister could speak direct to the President of the United States; and nearby, in his sparsely furnished bedroom, Churchill could occasionally be persuaded to stay overnight if raids were particularly severe.

The Map Room of the Cabinet War Rooms was manned day and night throughout the Second World War.

The ivory telephone was a direct line to #10 Downing Street.

Above: Most Prime Ministers have used #10 Downing Street as their private as well as official residence. Left: The Cenotaph is close to the junction of WHITEHALL and its southern extension, Parliament Street.

#10 Downing Street This apparently insignificant address, known throughout the world as the official London residence of the Prime Minister, is an allegory for British reserve and understatement. This house is larger inside than outside. According to Pevsner it 'deceives ninety-nine out of a hundred'. Behind its narrow brick façade is an extensive complex of government offices, official reception rooms and private apartments. In fact #10, #11 and #12 Downing Street are all internally interconnected. #10 contains the Cabinet Room and the Prime Minister's offices; #11 is the official residence of the Chancellor of the Exchequer; and #12 houses the government's Party Whips' office.

Cenotaph (from the Greek *kenos* = empty and *taphos* = tomb) A monument to the Glorious Dead of two world wars, the lines of the Cenotaph are neither horizontal nor vertical in evocation of infinity: the apparent horizontals are convex around a common centre c274m below ground; the apparent verticals converge to a point c305m above ground. Erected in 1920, it was designed in Portland stone by Sir Edwin Lutyens. Each year a ceremony, held at 11am on the Sunday nearest the eleventh day of the eleventh month, is attended by royalty, leading politicians and representatives of the fighting forces of much of the Commonwealth.

Ministry of Defence Today the east side of WHITEHALL is dominated by a monumental modern structure designed in 1957 to house the Ministry of Defence and over 5000 civil servants. Of the £5 million construction costs, £100,000 went towards the preservation of Henry VIII's Wine Cellar, now incarcerated deep below this modern massif. This astonishingly large, brick-vaulted chamber, 21m long by 9m wide, was encased in concrete, winched slowly 13m to one side and lowered bodily 6m into a specially excavated cavity.

Banqueting House Designed in Portland stone by Inigo Jones in 1622, this outstanding model of Palladian architecture is the principal survivor of WHITEHALL Palace. It replaced an earlier banqueting hall at a cost of £15,653 3s 3d and was opened with a masque by Ben Johnson. Charles I frequently held lavish banquets here and commissioned Rubens to design the nine luxurious ceiling paintings. Yet it was to this building that Charles walked for the last time across St James's Park one bitter January morning in 1649. Out through a window he stepped, to a temporary scaffold where an uncertain crowd watched the headsman's sharp axe despatch this sad and final absolute monarch.

Horse Guards Descended from an original small guardhouse built here in Henry VIII's tilt yard, this attractive stone building (Kent and Vardy 1750-8) is today the office of the Commander in Chief of the combined forces. Outside, on the WHITEHALL frontage, two troopers sit motionless astride their immaculately groomed mounts – in strange contradistinction to the dust and frenzy of those ancient tilting tournaments attended by knights from all over Europe. Behind, stretching between WHITEHALL and St James's Park, is **Horse Guards Parade**, the site of the original tilt yard proper. Here is conducted each June the Trooping the Colour, the monarch's spectacular official birthday parade.

'A view of the Horse Guards from Whitehall.'

Great Scotland Yard The name by which Britain's police headquarters are known across the world is derived from a former warren of yards and alleyways at the north-east end of WHITEHALL. By the 17thC part of the old Palace of WHITEHALL was known as Scotland Yard, Middle Scotland Yard and Inner Scotland Yard. (The story that this area had been used by kings of Scotland paying homage to kings of England may well be English propaganda.) In 1829 Sir Robert Peel's new Metropolitan Police Force set up its first headquarters here. Although since then the 'Yard' has moved twice, in 1883 to Cannon Row and in 1967 to Victoria Street, its evocative title remains – shorthand the world over for the highest standards of criminal investigation.

Famous people

Thomas Wolsey (c1475-1530), the butcher's son 'of low origin' who rose to supreme power under Henry VIII and lavishly improved York Place, possessed considerable estates and properties throughout England, including the attractive Hampton Court Palace. All of these he forfeited in 1529 when Henry lost patience with his favoured cardinal for bungling his divorce from Catherine of Aragon. By the following year the broken ex-cardinal was dead, perishing on 29 November after arrest on charges of high treason.

King Henry VIII (1491-1547), who confiscated York Place and renamed it WHITEHALL, was, on his succession to the throne, a handsome and popular king – 'much handsomer than any other sovereign in Christendom'. By the time of his death thirty-eight years later he had the reputation of a cruel and bloody tyrant. In those grim years he had married six times, suppressed the Roman Catholic Church, made himself 'on earth supreme head of the Church of England', broken up the monasteries and beheaded countless notables, including two of his own wives.

King Charles I (1600-49) was the last absolute monarch of Britain following defeat in the bloody Civil War. Born so ill that he could barely talk or walk before the age of seven, he nevertheless grew to become a skilled horseman and consummate scholar. Denying its jurisdiction, he three times refused to plead before the self-styled court which tried 'the tyrant, traitor and murderer Charles Stuart'; and on a wind-torn scaffold in WHITEHALL he faced courageously the executioner about to behead his king, uttering finally the solitary word: 'Remember!'

Oliver Cromwell (1599-1658), Member of Parliament for Huntingdon who rose to oust and dispose of Charles I, became self-made 'Protector' and nearly accepted a kingship. He lived and died in WHITEHALL Palace. Within three years of his death his body had been exhumed, hung on the gallows at Tyburn and decapitated – the head being displayed on a pole above Westminster Hall.

Sir Winston Leonard Spencer Churchill (1874-1965), soldier, writer, orator, statesman and British prime minister, is inextricably associated with WHITEHALL and the Second World War. Displaying little talent as a schoolboy, he followed an eventful military spell with a dazzling and meteoric entry into political life. This was but preparation for his 'walk with destiny' when, at the age of 65, he accepted the office of prime minister and offered nothing but 'blood, toil, tears and sweat' in his resolute determination to combat the forces of Fascism. From a microphone at #10 Downing Street Churchill would broadcast to the nation and beyond, his unmistakable voice inspiring a war-torn Europe.

Popular associations: Smart hotels / Sherlock Holmes

NORTHUMBERLAND AVENUE

(WC2/City of Westminster)

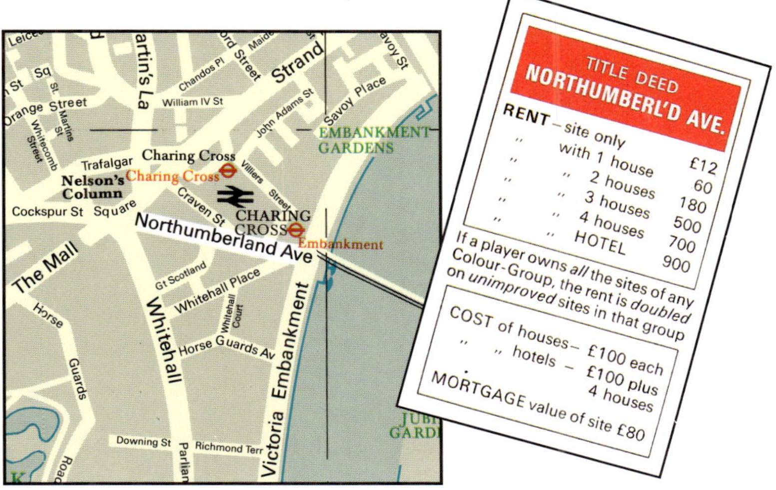

MONOPOLY valuation: £160
Current valuation: £84,000,000

Location description

A broad avenue of less than 300m between Charing Cross and the Victoria Embankment, originally famous for its smart hotels but now containing mainly offices and other commercial buildings.

Derivation of name

NORTHUMBERLAND AVENUE takes its name from the house demolished for its construction: Northumberland House, one of the finest Jacobean buildings in England, London home of the Earls of Northumberland.

Short history

In about 1605 Henry Howard, Earl of Northampton, built himself an imposing castellated mansion at the extreme west end of the STRAND. Designed by Jansen and Christmas, it fronted the STRAND but had two wings running back towards the Thames. It was the last of a string of noblemen's palaces between STRAND and river. From his windows Northampton had a spectacular view across the gardens towards the river beyond. Yet he was unable to enjoy his new home for long, for he died in 1614. Eventually the house passed by marriage to Algernon Percy, 10th Earl of Northumberland. In 1749 a huge stone Percy lion was perched on a plinth over the Strand gateway; and a ballroom and art gallery were added. By the middle of the 1800s Northumberland House had been engulfed by shops and commercial buildings. Immediately in front of it TRAFALGAR SQUARE had been laid out; behind, the Thames embankments were under construction. Reluctantly, the duke sold the property in 1873 for £500,000 to the Metropolitan Board of

Works who planned a major road improvement scheme. The structure was razed to the ground and the great Percy lion taken to Syon House at Isleworth. Across the foundations of house and garden, between the Strand and the newly built Victoria Embankment, NORTHUMBERLAND AVENUE was laid out in 1876.

Above: General view of NORTHUMBERLAND AVENUE. Right: The Royal Commonwealth Society exists to promote an understanding of what the Commonwealth stands for.

Points of interest

Playhouse Theatre In 1882 the speculator Sefton Parry built the Avenue Theatre on the east side of NORTHUMBERLAND AVENUE. This theatre staged many important productions including Shaw's first showing of *Arms and the Man* in 1894 and 544 performances of *A Message from Mars* in 1899. In 1905 part of the neighbouring Charing Cross Station collapsed on the theatre killing six people. Virtually destroyed, it was rebuilt to run successfully as the Playhouse Theatre until becoming a BBC studio in 1951.

Royal Commonwealth Society (#18) Founded as the Royal Colonial Institute in 1868 to reinforce ties between Britain and her colonies, its first elected Fellow was the Australian newspaper tycoon Edward Wilson. In 1885 the Institute chose NORTHUMBERLAND AVENUE for its headquarters. Rebuilt in 1936, damaged by bombs in 1941 and reconstructed in 1957, its panelled rooms house the world's finest collection of woods from all over the Commonwealth. It became the Royal Commonwealth Society in 1958, with a current membership of over 20,000 and an impressive library containing half a million items.

Famous people

Henry Howard, Earl of Northampton (c1539-1614), whose poet father was beheaded at the age of thirty by Henry VIII, was the creator of Northumberland House. Shortly before his own death he was implicated in the murder of Sir Thomas Overbury who had said of his relative, the beautiful but profligate Frances Howard, that she might do for a mistress but not for a wife.

Algernon Percy, 10th Earl of Northumberland (1602-68), whose forefather had accompanied William the Conqueror to England, fought first against and then for Charles I. During the Civil War Charles I's children were put into his charge and to Northumberland House leading royalists came secretly to plot the restoration of the monarchy.

'I am delighted that you have come down, Mr Holmes.'

Sherlock Holmes (1854-c1957) had important connections with NORTHUMBERLAND AVENUE. It was here at the Northumberland Hotel in 1898 that Sir Henry Baskerville (born c1859) stayed on coming to London to consult the great detective in Conan Doyle's *Hound of the Baskervilles*. This hotel is now the Sherlock Holmes public house (#10 Northumberland Street), with an intriguing collection of Holmesiana and a reconstruction of Holmes's front room at #221b Baker Street.

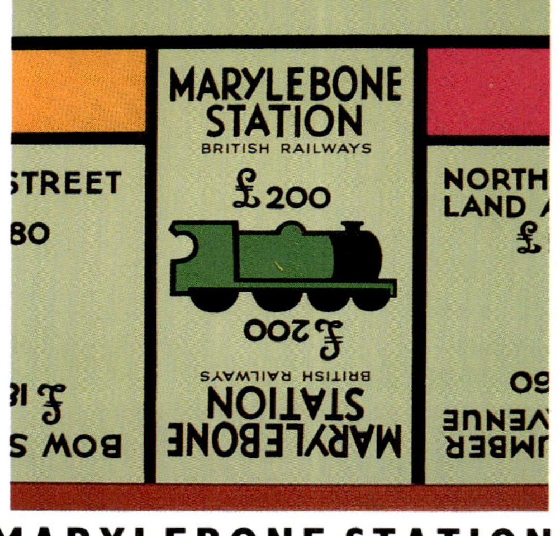

MARYLEBONE STATION

(Marylebone Road, NW1/City of Westminster)

Small and friendly terminus of British Rail's London Midland Region, MARYLEBONE STATION is the most westerly site on the MONOPOLY board.

MONOPOLY valuation: £200
Current valuation: £90,000,000

Opening date

1899

Principal destinations

Include Aylesbury, Banbury and High Wycombe

Traffic statistics

Passenger trains daily: 110
Passengers daily: 15,000

Station background

In the days when a network of private Victorian railways competed vigorously for the most succulent traffic, the seeds of romantic MARYLEBONE STATION were sown in far away Grimsby. From this bustling fishing port on England's north-east coast, the lines of the Manchester Sheffield and Lincolnshire Railway struggled across country to Manchester via Sheffield. Unprofitable and impoverished, the MS & LR had relinquished the more lucrative London traffic – until its imaginative chairman, the visionary Sir Edward William Watkin, became chairman too of the Metropolitan Railway in 1872. His sights set secretly on the proposed Channel tunnel, Watkin boldly resolved to carry the MS & LR to London, partly using the tracks of the Metropolitan. Yet his proposals of 1891 aroused formidable opposition from residents of St John's Wood and members of the sacred Marylebone Cricket Club at Lord's, across whose property the last two miles of track would pass. The savage two year struggle, and the expensive tunnelling that solved the problem, almost cost the MS & LR its remaining solvency and Watkin his health. Then, in 1897, the company's provincial sounding title was felt inappropriate to a company whose tracks passed beneath the hallowed sods of St John's Wood; from 1 August the MS & LR became the more assertive Great Central Railway.

Having exhausted its funds, the GCR contented itself with a terminus humble by comparison to KING'S CROSS STATION or LIVERPOOL STREET STATION. No architect could be afforded, the 'architectural details' being left to one of the company's engineers. Its locomotives and coaches could be obtained only under hire purchase. And the inevitable station hotel, so often the railway's *piéce de résistance,* became the responsibility of another company. In fact the architect-designed 700-bedroom, seven-storey Hotel Great Central, fully equipped with rooftop cycle track, dwarfed and obliterated the station it served.

Although coaches from modern MARYLEBONE STATION do carry more than the four passengers of the 1899 opening train, the lucrative traffic that Watkins envisaged never really materialised. Perhaps because of these difficulties, MARYLEBONE STATION today has a genteel aura unique among the London termini. With its plethora of 'GCR' motifs, its wide, empty platforms and its generous capacity, much in demand by film makers seeking expansive railway locations, MARYLEBONE STATION remains a fantasy that has never quite shaken off the quiet, provincial flavour of that original line from Grimsby.

Above: From the start an elegant iron and glass *porte-cochère* spanned the space between station and hotel.
Left: 'GCR' motifs abound.

Station timetable

1899 (9 March): inauguration of new MARYLEBONE STATION passenger terminus, the last main-line station to be built in London; 700 guests entertained to luncheon in a decorated train.

1899 (15 March): public service commences with first train leaving MARYLEBONE STATION at 5.15am carrying only four passengers.

1899 (1 July): Hotel Great Central opens to public.

1913: Leicester express collides with High Wycombe train, killing one passenger.

1914-18 (First World War): Army mail trains servicing Army Mail Office in nearby Regent's Park use MARYLEBONE STATION extensively. Hotel Great Central requisitioned by Government as convalescent home for wounded officers.

1939-45 (Second World War): little serious damage inflicted by enemy incendiary bombs. MARYLEBONE STATION closed 5 October-26 November 1940 as result of bomb damage to approach tunnel. Signalbox damaged by flying bomb towards end of war; two signalmen killed. Hotel Great Central again requisitioned.

1928.

Popular associations: Police / Magistrates' Court / BOW STREET Runners

BOW STREET

(WC2/City of Westminster)

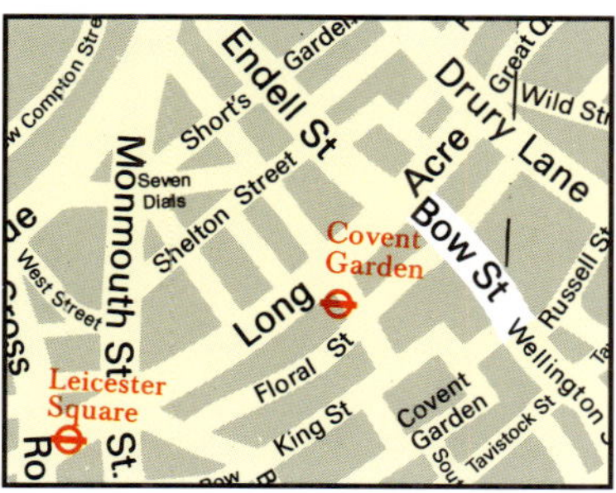

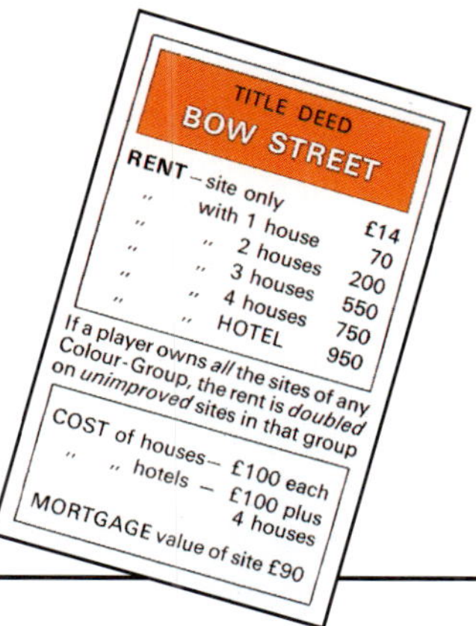

MONOPOLY valuation: £180
Current valuation: £60,000,000

Location description

Running between Russell Street and Long Acre just north of the STRAND, BOW STREET plays host to connoisseurs of opera and ballet on one side and defenders of law and order on the other. The street borders Covent Garden, an area of earthy vitality and traditional hub of London's theatreland.

Derivation of name

BOW STREET originally took its name from its demure little curve in an otherwise straight composition.

Short history

Laid out between 1633 and 1677, BOW STREET was originally a respectable address 'resorted unto by gentry for lodgings'. By the mid-18thC the tone of the area was in decline, with eight licensed premises in the street. From c1760 *Harris's List of Covent Garden Ladies,* definitive guide to the district's prostitutes, was published annually. And by the early-19thC BOW STREET itself was notorious for bordellos.

Points of interest

BOW STREET Magistrates' Court In 1740 the first BOW STREET magistrate, Colonel Sir Thomas De Veil, set up court in his home on the west side of BOW STREET. He was succeeded by the barrister Henry Fielding, already famous as a novelist and dramatist. Henry's blind half-brother John assisted him, becoming the third BOW STREET magistrate in 1754. The courthouse was rebuilt in 1880 at its present site on the east side. Today it is the Chief Metropolitan Magistrates' Court, and its three courtrooms witness a curious blend of prosecutions, including all extradition proceedings which must be heard here before the Metropolitan Chief Magistrate.

The present BOW STREET Magistrates' Court, opposite the Royal Opera House, was completed at a cost of just over £38,000 in 1880.

BOW STREET Runners Henry Fielding considered the contemporary system of parish constables and watchmen inadequate. To the horror of Londoners he organized a mobile squad of six part-time 'thief-takers' who wore no uniform and sometimes worked freelance. From this group the BOW STREET Runners developed, predecessors of Sir Robert Peel's Metropolitan Police Force of 1829. Foot squads patrolled up to six kilometres out of London. From there scarlet-waistcoated horse patrols ('Robin Redbreasts') would patrol a further twenty-five kilometres. The BOW STREET Runners themselves were finally disbanded in 1839.

BOW STREET Police Station (#28) is marked unusually by two ornately mounted white globes. The customary blue police light distressed Queen Victoria when visiting the Royal Opera opposite, supposedly because her beloved Prince Albert had died in the Blue Room at Windsor. At her command it was changed to white. The **Metropolitan Police Historical Museum** was for years housed in the police station, telling the story of London's police force with uniforms, photographs, books and documents. In 1983 lack of space caused it to be mothballed, with the intention of opening a larger museum at Wapping in 1989.

The **Royal Opera House** ('Covent Garden' in art-criticese) is undoubtedly one of the world's premier venues for opera and ballet. Within this huge theatre, celebrated for its flawless acoustics, over 2000 devotees of musical drama can listen regularly to the world's most distinguished artistes. The present building, completed in 1858, is the third on this site. The first theatre, dating from 1732, burned down in 1808, destroying Händel's organ and many of his manuscripts. The second suffered a similar fate in 1856.

Covent Garden Market was, until 1974 when it moved to Battersea, famous as London's nocturnal fresh fruit and vegetable market from which wholesale produce was daily despatched countrywide. Its name is a corruption of the ancient 5,6ha 'convent garden' which stretched from Long Acre to the Strand as early as 1200. Before Henry VIII it belonged to the monks of the Abbey of St Peter, Westminster. In 1536 the property was granted to the Russell family, Earls of Bedford, who developed the area and encouraged the creation of the market. Much of the 17thC Italianate development and Piazza by Inigo Jones has gone, but the later Victorian buildings have been attractively restored and now accommodate a variety of fascinating small shops, coffee houses, boutiques, studios and promenades.

Above: Both the Royal Opera and the Royal Ballet perform at the Royal Opera House, with its colonnaded façade in BOW STREET and its box office just around the corner in Floral Street.
Right: Covent Garden Market today.

Theatre Royal Drury Lane Just off BOW STREET, in Catherine Street, is the illustrious 300-year old Theatre Royal Drury Lane where many eminent actors like David Garrick and Mrs Siddons made their débuts. In 1840 the walled-up skeleton of a man complete with rib-clasped knife was discovered. It is assumed to be the ghost of this luckless man that haunts the upper circle during matinée performances.

Famous people

Claude Duval (1643-70), the gentlemanly highwayman who 'danced a gavot with the ladies', probably lies buried in the 'actors' church' of St Paul Covent Garden (Inigo Place). This French gallant pursued a successful if short-lived career as a knight of the road on the outskirts of London. Intoxicated with alcohol on one occasion, he was captured, convicted and hanged at the age of twenty-seven. His epitaph succinctly records his exploits:

'Here lies Du Vall: Reader, if male thou art
Look to thy purse: if female to thy heart.'

Nell Gwynne (c1650-1687), actress and royal paramour born at Hereford, at first sold oranges in Covent Garden. Later she became a popular comedienne in nearby Drury Lane where Charles II met and fell in love with her. By him she had at least one son and probably a second. Ever faithful to Charles's memory, she rejected one contender with the words: 'Shall the dog lie where the deer once crouched?'

Grinling Gibbons (1648-1721), famous sculptor and master carver to the kings Charles II to George I, at one time lived in BOW STREET.

Henry Fielding (1707-54), the second BOW STREET magistrate, was also a highly successful novelist and playwright. His first play, *Love in Several Masques*, was premièred at Drury Lane. His greatest novel, *The History of Tom Jones* published in 1749 and successfully filmed in 1962, has become a literary classic.

Sir John Fielding (d1780), lawyer, was the half-brother of Henry Fielding whom he assisted and then succeeded. Blinded in a childhood accident, and said to have been able to recognise 3,000 thieves by their voices, he was knighted in 1761 for his work at BOW STREET.

COMMUNITY CHEST

DOCTOR'S FEE PAY £50

Did you know . . . that the earliest major European operation under anaesthesia was in London? After amputating a patient's leg in 1846, Robert Liston, who had heard of anaesthesia in America, announced to his watching students: 'This yankee dodge, gentlemen, beats mesmerism hollow.'

GO TO JAIL
MOVE DIRECTLY TO JAIL DO NOT PASS "GO"
DO NOT COLLECT £200

Did you know . . . that in London's grim and notorious Fleet Prison clandestine marriages – since outlawed – used to be contracted without licence, usually by imprisoned clergymen?

PAY HOSPITAL £100

Did you know . . . that the world 'bedlam' – defined by the *Concise Oxford Dictionary* as 'scene of uproar' – is derived from the ancient Bethlehem Royal Hospital, once used as a lunatic asylum and now the site of LIVERPOOL STREET STATION?

YOU INHERIT £100

Did you know . . . that in 1855 Thomas Cubitt, early speculative builder responsible for much of MAYFAIR, left £1,000,000 in what was then the longest will ever recorded?

PAY A £10 FINE OR TAKE A "CHANCE"

Did you know . . . that Lloyd's of London once fined the chairman of one of its syndicates £1,000,000 in connection with alleged misappropriation of nearly £40,000,000?

RECEIVE INTEREST ON 7% PREFERENCE SHARES £25

Did you know . . . that in his famous *Dictionary* Dr Johnson defined the 18thC London stockbroker as: 'a low wretch who makes money by buying and selling shares in funds'?

MARLBOROUGH STREET

(W1/City of Westminster)

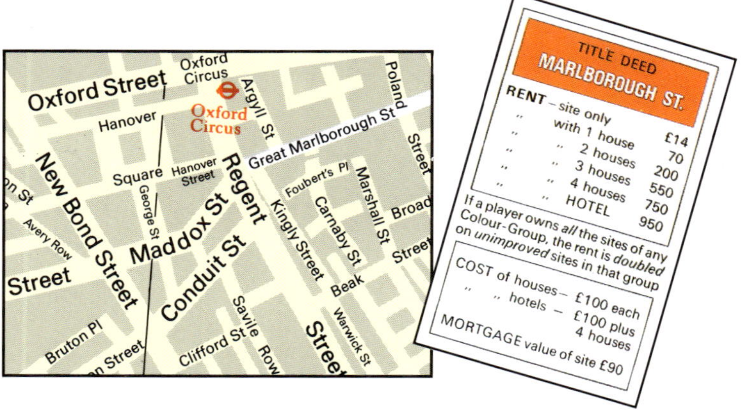

MONOPOLY valuation: £180
Current valuation: £45,200,000

Location description

Great MARLBOROUGH STREET is known by local people simply as MARLBOROUGH STREET (not to be confused with the street of the same name in SW3). A broad avenue running parallel to and just south of OXFORD STREET, today it links REGENT STREET to Poland Street. Like the other two orange MONOPOLY sites, MARLBOROUGH STREET has had strong associations with the Police.

"And everybody praised the Duke,
Who this great fight did win.'
'But what good came of it at last?'
Quoth little Peterkin.
'Why that I cannot tell,' said he,
'But 'twas a famous victory."
Robert Southey (1774-1843)
The Battle of Blenheim

Derivation of name

The street was named after John Churchill, 1st Duke of Marlborough and legendary English general.

Short history

On 13 August 1704 the Duke of Marlborough convincingly defeated French troops near the small Bavarian village of Blenheim, killing, wounding and capturing nearly 40,000 of the opposing forces. MARLBOROUGH STREET was laid out a few years later and so named in commemoration of the victorious duke. It was reputed to be one of the finest streets in Europe, largely because of its great breadth and attractive gardens. Originally residential, it immediately attracted occupants of 'prime quality', including peers of the realm and distinguished scientists and doctors.

The **London Palladium**, in Argyll Street just off MARLBOROUGH STREET, was built on the site of the Duke of Marlborough's former town house. This famous music-hall opened in 1910 at a cost of £250,000, its box-to-box telephones and Norwegian granite palm-court making it one of the most lavish theatres of its day. Noted for the great scale and spectacle of its revues, it soon became Mecca to aspiring vaudeville artists at home and abroad. Today the London Palladium stages the pick of variety shows, the annual Royal Command Performance and Christmas pantomimes.

The **Dog & Trumpet** public house (#37) used to be until recently the Marlborough Head which had been on this site since 1739. The **Coach & Horses** public house (#1) has also been here from 1739.

The present **Magistrates' Court** (#21), still in use today as a stipendiary court, was built in 1913. Next to it is a disused police station. A parish watch house had existed in MARLBOROUGH STREET from as early as 1793, and in 1900, according to *Police Orders,* 'the new station at Great Marlborough-street was taken into occupation and business commenced therein'. (This was closed in 1940 when business was transferred to West End Central Police Station in Savile Row.) Nearby, an 18thC anatomist, Joshua Brookes, maintained a museum in which he used to exhibit the bodies of criminals, many of whom had been both caught and sentenced in MARLBOROUGH STREET.

Points of interest

Liberty and Company Ltd (#210/220 Regent Street) At the west end of Great MARLBOROUGH STREET, at the junction with REGENT STREET, the immaculately dressed windows of Liberty's department store display clothes and materials of the finest quality. 'Liberty print' as a fabric design has won favour around the world. But of the 1923 store's 'Tudor' façade the architectural purist might despair. Authentic man-of-war oaken timbers, hand-made roofing tiles, stained and leaded windows – nothing can assuage the scathing comments of Nikolaus Pevsner: 'The scale is wrong, the symmetry is wrong . . . and the goings-on of a store behind such a façade are wrongest of all.'

Palladium House (#1/4 Argyll Street), a uniquely stark, black, Egyptian-flavoured granite building faces Liberty's incongruously from across MARLBOROUGH STREET. Known originally as Ideal House, having been built and occupied by the heating engineers Ideal Standard, it was designed in 1928 by the American architect Raymond Hood whose American Radiator Building in New York was similar in style. Today Palladium House is an exclusive office complex for various professional and commercial businesses.

The **London College of Music** (#47) was founded in 1887 to satisfy the Victorians' insatiable appetite for musical facilities and education.

Little MARLBOROUGH STREET John Rocque's map of 1747 demonstrates the esteem in which the Duke of Marlborough was held. Great MARLBOROUGH STREET, laid out before the construction of REGENT STREET, stops at 'Argyle (now Argyll) Street'. Just south, Little MARLBOROUGH STREET runs into 'King (now Kingly) Street'; just off Carnaby Street is 'Marlborough or Carnaby Market' and 'Marlborough Row'; while to the north is 'Marlborough Mewse', crossed by 'Blenheim Street'. Even though the last two have been renamed, they still have connections with Marlborough: Ramillies Place and Ramillies Street both commemorate one of the Duke's resounding victories when he repulsed Louis XIV's forces at the little Belgian village of Ramillies in 1706.

Carnaby Street, just south of Great MARLBOROUGH STREET, no longer has the modish, world-famous aura that it acquired in the swinging '60s, but retains its place in the *Concise Oxford Dictionary* where it is defined as: 'Fashionable clothing for young people'. It pre-dates Great MARLBOROUGH STREET, having been laid out in the 1680s. In 1683 Richard Tyler, a bricklayer turned property developer, built a house here which he called Karnaby House, although the derivation is unclear.

Famous people

John Churchill, 1st Duke of Marlborough (1650-1722), commemorated by Great MARLBOROUGH STREET and surrounding area, was the son of Sir Winston Churchill. From impecunious beginnings he rose to achieve supreme command of the British forces. For his brilliant generalship and succession of military victories a grateful nation showered gifts upon him, including his dukedom and palatial residence at Woodstock. Yet the last years of his life were soured by political intrigue and humiliation. Falsely accused of embezzling Army funds, he was deprived of his command and publicly abused. Four years later however, on the accession of George I in 1714, he was restored to full honours and organised the defence of the kingdom against the Jacobite uprising.

Henry Cavendish (1731-1810), the great scientist known as the 'Newton of chemistry', lived in Great MARLBOROUGH STREET for several years. He was a solitary man who gave standing orders to his female servants to keep out of sight, ordering his dinner daily by placing a note on the hall table.

Sarah Siddons (1755-1831), the tragic actress who bedazzled London audiences with her Lady Macbeth, was a resident of Great MARLBOROUGH STREET for fourteen years at the height of her success. Possibly unequalled as a tragic actress at any time or in any country, she was a stunning and queenly figure with a voice of great energy and flexibility.

Horatio Nelson (1758-1805), one-eyed, one-armed Admiral of the Fleet, viscount and national hero, lodged at #10 Great MARLBOROUGH STREET for a while after his marriage in 1787 to Mrs Nisbett. His romantic extra-marital liaison with the bewitching Lady Hamilton was concluded only by his premature death from enemy fire during the Battle of Trafalgar.

Charles Robert Darwin (1809-82), naturalist, lived in Great MARLBOROUGH STREET for two years following his circumnavigation of the globe in HMS *Beagle* from 1831-1836. From this long expedition Darwin acquired the detailed knowledge for his *Origin of Species* that was so radically to reorientate scientific and religious opinion when published in 1859.

VINE STREET

(W1/City of Westminster)

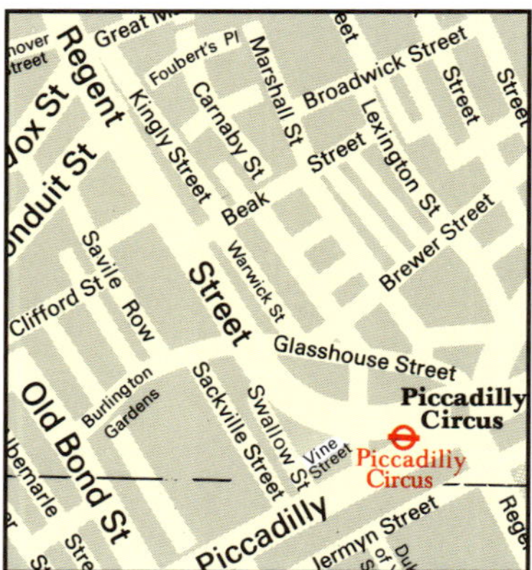

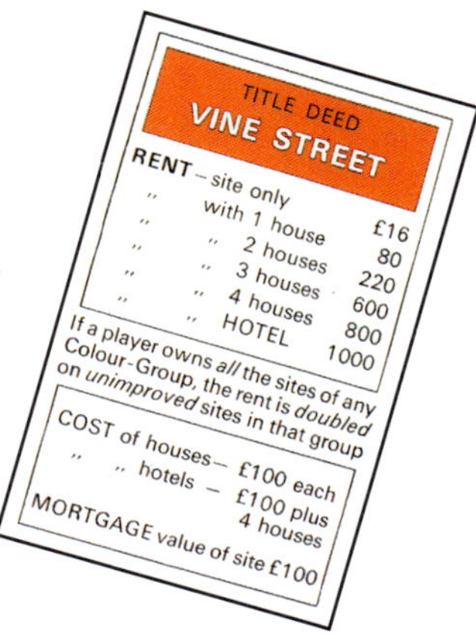

MONOPOLY valuation: £200
Current valuation: £7,200,000

Location description

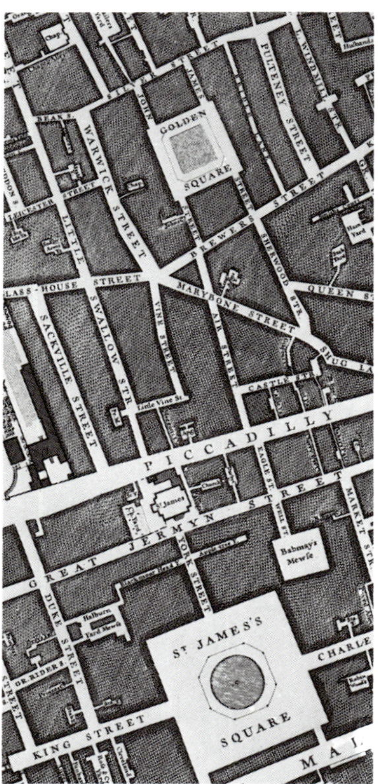

John Rocque map of London 1747.

VINE STREET is the shortest and narrowest of all the streets on the MONOPOLY board, and the only true cul-de-sac. At the extreme east end of PICCADILLY, the delightfully narrow Swallow Street links PICCADILLY with REGENT STREET. At its centre is tiny VINE STREET, a vigorous offshoot pruned well back. In the 18thC this was a longer, open-ended street. Today, hemmed in and dwarfed by the later buildings that tower above it, it seems little more than a parking lot for the evocative-sounding VINE STREET Police Station that extends along most of its length.

Derivation of name

VINE STREET took its name from the Vine Inn which was a landmark of the street in the early-18thC.

Short history

By the time of John Rocque's stunning 1747 map of London, the foundations of today's VINE STREET were clear. Swallow Street ran north from PICCADILLY to OXFORD STREET. Off Swallow Street, Little VINE STREET struggled a valiant 50m east before turning abruptly north and continuing as VINE STREET to Warwick Street. REGENT STREET, the great thoroughfare that Nash and the Prince Regent were to smash through VINE STREET and along the length of Swallow Street, did not yet exist. The Ordnance Survey map of 1869 reveals the aftermath of the REGENT STREET adventure: a shattered VINE STREET lies in two halves, now called Great VINE STREET to the north and VINE STREET to the south; between them, the phalanx of the REGENT STREET Quadrant; to their west a truncated Swallow Street. By 1894, Great VINE STREET had lost ground to Warwick Street, and all that remained to honour its memory was today's tiny VINE STREET cul-de-sac south of the Quadrant.

Above: The Vine public house in PICCADILLY Place recalls the 18thC inn that gave its name to VINE STREET.

Below: Swallow Street.

The police station occupies virtually the entire northern flank of modern VINE STREET.

Points of interest

VINE STREET Police Station (#10) In September 1829 the first Metropolitan policemen donned their stylish blue uniforms. At #10 Little VINE STREET six of them settled in to the old parish watch house, redesignated the official police station. By 1856 #9 and #11 had been absorbed, creating a small courtroom and reflecting the station's growing status. There has been a police connection here ever since, although the present building is not original. In 1939 VINE STREET and MARLBOROUGH STREET Police Stations were both relocated as West End Central in Savile Row. The name VINE STREET was discarded in favour of PICCADILLY Place and the site used first as the Aliens' Registration Office and later as a base for murder squads. In 1971 the site was reactivated as a police station, becoming VINE STREET once again at the prompting of a nostalgic police commissioner who had served here as a young constable.

Man in Moon Passage is a narrow walk-through linking VINE STREET to the REGENT STREET Quadrant. There had been a Man-in-the-Moon pub at this spot since the early-1700s, but in 1931 this too was absorbed into the overflowing police station.

Piccadilly Place is today a brief pedestrian alleyway between VINE STREET and PICCADILLY. For a time VINE STREET too was known as PICCADILLY Place. The Vine public house in this passage recalls the original inn from which VINE STREET derived its name.

Swallow Street Tucked away between REGENT STREET and PICCADILLY, the pizza shops, wine bars and sandwich counters of the colourful if abbreviated Swallow Street lend the vicinity an air of Continental charm. Built in 1671, it took its name from Thomas Swallow who leased land here from the Crown in the mid-16thC. Today, only Swallow Passage and Swallow Place 800m to the north testify to Swallow Street's original length.

Famous people

Mary Richardson, young suffragette who assaulted and slashed Velazquez's *Toilet of Venus* in the National Gallery off nearby TRAFALGAR SQUARE in 1914, was taken to VINE STREET Police Station after her arrest. 'Slasher Mary', as she became known, announced that in assailing the canvas of the celebrated oil painting – then worth £45,000 – she was attacking the men who 'gaped all day' at the recumbent, nude Venus. At the time of the assault, Mary Richardson was on release from Holloway Prison to recover from a hunger strike. The 17thC canvas was successfully restored at modest expense; but owing to differential rates of fading the wounds to the hip and back can now be seen in certain lights.

Left: 'Slasher Mary' leaves VINE STREET Police Station for appearance in court on Tuesday 10 March 1914, following her mutilation of the Velazquez canvas (above).

VINE STREET

REGENT STREET £300
GO TO
PICCADILLY £280
WATER WORKS
£150
COVENTRY STREET £260
LEICESTER SQUARE £260
FENCHURCH ST STATION
BRITISH RAILWAYS
£200
MONOPOLY
100
500
DEED
STRAND
RENT – site only £18
with 1 house 90
2 houses 250
3 houses 700
4 houses 875
HOTEL 1050
If a player owns all the sites of any Colour-Group, the rent is doubled on unimproved sites in that group
COST of houses – £150 each
hotels – £150 plus 4 houses
MORTGAGE value of site £110

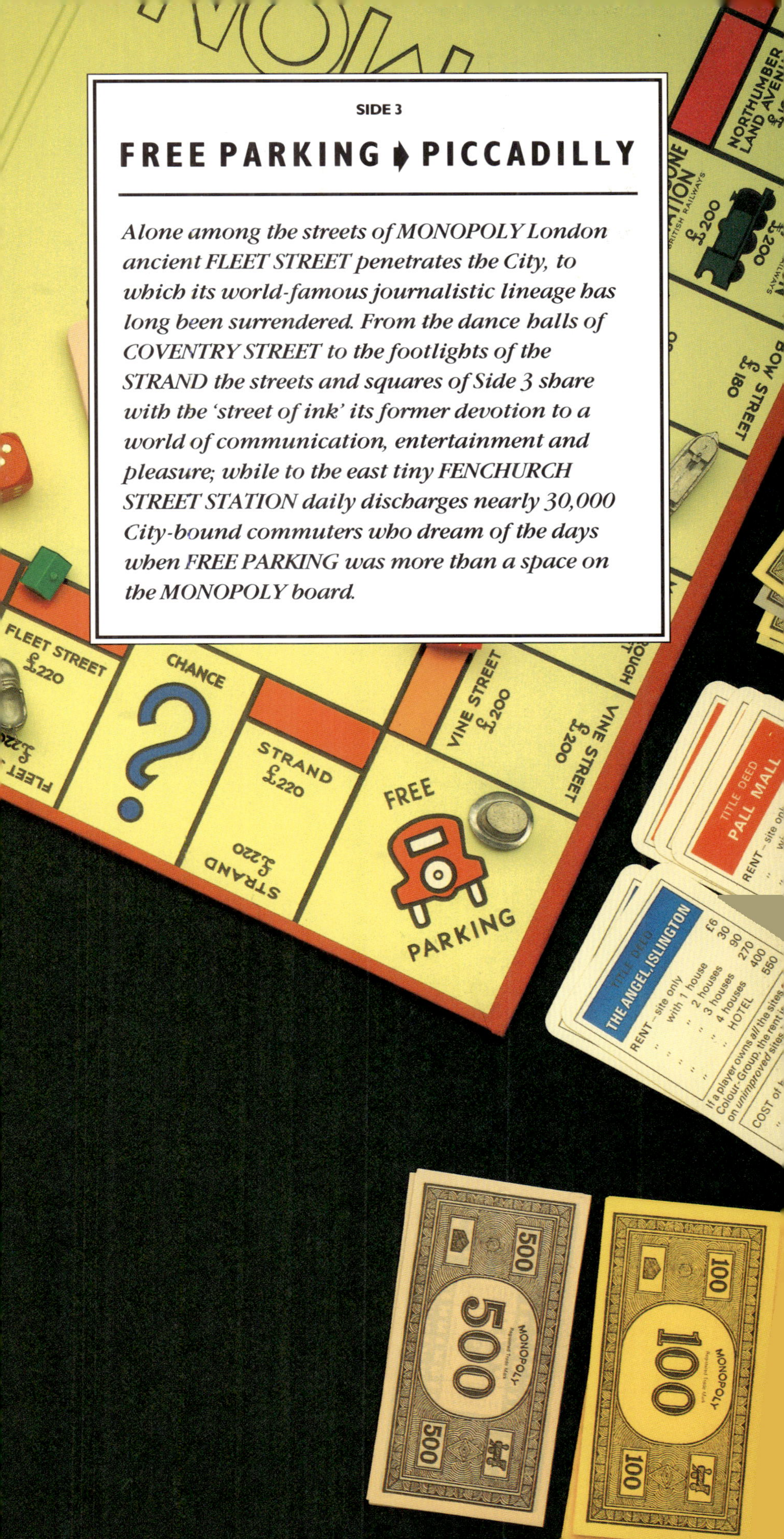

SIDE 3

FREE PARKING ▸ PICCADILLY

Alone among the streets of MONOPOLY London ancient FLEET STREET penetrates the City, to which its world-famous journalistic lineage has long been surrendered. From the dance halls of COVENTRY STREET to the footlights of the STRAND the streets and squares of Side 3 share with the 'street of ink' its former devotion to a world of communication, entertainment and pleasure; while to the east tiny FENCHURCH STREET STATION daily discharges nearly 30,000 City-bound commuters who dream of the days when FREE PARKING was more than a space on the MONOPOLY board.

FREE PARKING

Transport in London

'To travel hopefully is a better thing than to arrive . . .'

Robert Louis Stevenson (1850-1894)

FREE PARKING in central London may be a privilege enjoyed exclusively by MONOPOLY players and monarchs; but traffic jams and city congestion are certainly not unique to the 20thC.

When in AD410 the last Roman legions pulled out of Britain, London was at the hub of a sophisticated network of national roads. Yet it was to be the River Thames which would be the primary means of transport within the early capital.

For many centuries the horse ferry just upstream from Westminster plied the Thames, tolls going to the Archbishops of Canterbury whose palace at Lambeth may be seen on the right. In this early-18thC painting St Paul's Cathedral may be seen in the distance.

Probing more than 50km inland, the river was an important avenue for international sea traffic, delivering cargoes and passengers to the very heart of the kingdom. For Londoners too it was a vital form of communication and movement, conveying passengers and commodities between City and Westminster. From their riverside gardens along the STRAND, noblemen and bishops could step effortlessly into private barges to be carried swiftly upstream to Court. To Traitor's Gate – watery portal of the Tower of London – hesitant guests were conveyed by boat. From the Thames-side palace at WHITEHALL monarchs would retreat for their country residences up and down the river. For centuries the Thames was a congested 'forest of masts', plied by countless river taxis and ferries, their watermen competing fiercely for custom: until eventually road challenged river, and steam supplanted what little oar was left.

Visscher's panoramic view of London in 1616 depicts 'Thamesis Fluvius' as a bustling and important thoroughfare. The Tower of London, London Bridge and old St Paul's can be clearly discerned.

Travel by road within London ever took various forms. From Roman times the horse was important, a sturdy mount for rider and motive power for cart or carriage. Litters, borne by horses or men, transported passengers up to mediaeval times. And in the 1500s the horse-drawn coach was introduced. Yet it was not until the early-1600s that the two-seater hackney-carriage launched public transport onto the roads of London – an advance vehemently opposed by the Thames watermen who correctly foresaw their own demise. By the turn of the 19thC an efficient intercity network of coaches was centred on London, with passengers boarding and alighting at bustling coaching inns like THE ANGEL ISLINGTON. Both the hackney-carriage (forebear of the modern taxi) and the Spanish sedan chair lost ground when George Shillibeer's horse-drawn omnibus ran – 'upon the Parisian mode' – along EUSTON ROAD in 1829. By this time London's roads were congested and dangerous, and the 1835 Highway Act was to make 'furious driving' a statutory offence. Nevertheless, Shillibeer's omnibus evolved successfully through the double-decker to the motor-bus of today; and in the 1860s came the trundling tramcar – a hybrid between train and bus which survived well into the mid-20thC.

Above and right: 200 years of modern transport in London are vividly captured at Covent Garden's London Transport Museum.

Early in the 19thC the railway age had introduced a new dimension into London's transportation system. Although the development of overground lines within central London was restricted, the railways conveyed thousands of commuters and visitors daily to and from the burgeoning capital. Within London, their natural extension was underground, the first such line running between Paddington and KING'S CROSS STATION in 1863 – and fairly soon developing into a comprehensive 'Tube' system which early employed electric rather than steam locomotives.

But it was to be the internal combustion engine that would reign supreme in the 20thC metropolis. The first horseless carriage had trotted onto the streets in 1895, and the Motor Car Act of 1903 introduced a system of licensing for drivers and raised the speed limit from 20km/h to 30km/h. Roads were improved with the London Traffic Act of 1924: hitherto, thirty-seven separate bodies had been free to dig up London's streets as and when they wished. The first fully automatic, three-colour traffic lights were installed at OXFORD STREET in 1931, and parking-meters followed in 1956 – at first only in MAYFAIR. In each twenty-four hour period some 2,500,000 vehicles now travel London's 14,000 tarred kilometres. Today, the capital is encircled by the world's longest bypass – the six-lane M25 orbital motorway; yet Britain's greatest traffic density at any one point may still be found at the south-west corner of MONOPOLY London where PARK LANE and PICCADILLY meet.

Popular associations: Theatres / hotels / stamp dealers

STRAND

(WC2/City of Westminster)

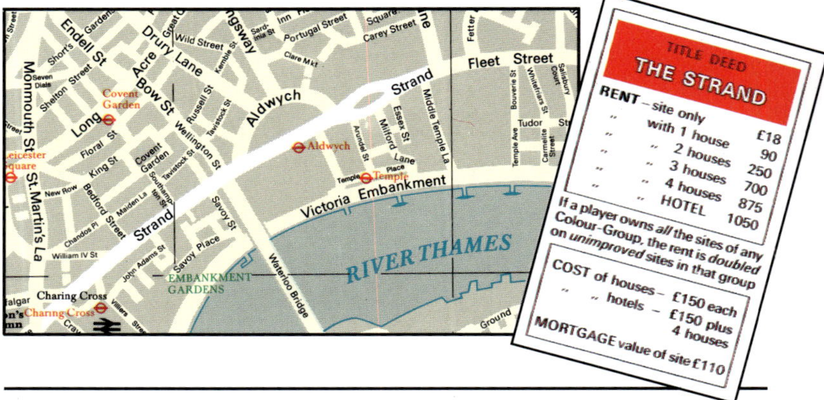

MONOPOLY valuation: £220

Current valuation: £702,000,000

Location description

'I walk down the STRAND
With my gloves on my hand
And I walk down again
With them off.'

William Hargreaves (d1941) ***Burlington Bertie***

1.3km in length, the STRAND today is a broad and busy thoroughfare linking TRAFALGAR SQUARE in the west to FLEET STREET in the east. This important route, originally the main road link between the Cities of London and Westminster, is no longer residential but a dense potpourri of varied shops, commercial offices, traditional restaurants, large hotels and Victorian theatres.

Derivation of name

The *Concise Oxford Dictionary* gives one definition of 'STRAND' as: 'Margin of sea, lake, or river, esp. foreshore.' London's STRAND was itself once a bridle-path lapped by the waters of the Thames, in the days when the river was wider than today and without embankment.

Short history

Mid-16thC maps of London depict the STRAND as an attractive, almost rural lane running beside the Thames. In those days the river brimmed with colourful boats and crested barges, a convenient means of travel between the larger, original City of London to the east and the smaller but developing City of Westminster to the west. Fine mansions and palaces lined its southern flank, their spacious gardens running down to the water's edge where steps and jetties led to waiting river-craft; while less imposing houses to the north looked out over green fields and open countryside. Even earlier, in the

12thC, there had been several elegant residences here on this important piece of real estate.

Right up to the 17thC the STRAND was lined with the mansions of bishops and nobles. By the mid-17thC new streets, shops and smaller, timber-framed houses, with nevertheless well-to-do and distinguished residents, were ousting the stately homes. In the 1700s came coffee houses, haunt of contemporary intelligentsia; ubiquitous sixpenny prostitutes with their 'enticing manner'; and swarming pickpockets, using their guile and enterprise to profit from the ever-bustling crowds.

In the 1830s following improvements by Nash to its west end, Disraeli was to describe the STRAND as 'perhaps the finest street in Europe'. Much redevelopment has since taken place, including the containment of the Thames by the Victoria Embankment, and little is left of its early beginnings. Yet in its adjoining streets and alleyways the past lives on: Arundel Street, Bedford Street, Durham House Street, Exeter Street, NORTHUMBERLAND AVENUE, Savoy Street — all echo the names of the holy, noble and powerful whose fine mansions once graced the shores of London's wide and lively waterway.

Somerset House rises sheer from a craft-laden Thames in this 18thC view looking upstream towards the York Watergate.

Savoy Palace was once the finest home in England. The Savoy Hotel, on the same site, is one of the finest hotels in the world.

Points of interest

Savoy Palace In the 13thC the stately home of the Count of Savoy was one of the most impressive residences along the STRAND. In the mid-14thC one of the count's successors, Henry, 1st Duke of Lancaster, grown wealthy with loot, spent a fortune adding a chapel, cloister and great hall, landscaping the grounds and stocking a fish-pool, making this home the finest in England. By 1381 it lay in ruins, smouldering victim of the Peasants' Revolt. Not until the early-16thC was it rebuilt, this time financed by a legacy in Henry VII's will as a hospital and almshouse complete with three chapels. Although again an impressive construction rising majestically from the Thames, it suffered from corrupt mismanagement and never flourished, the site eventually being substantially cleared in 1817 for the approach to the new Waterloo Bridge.

The **Queen's Chapel of the Savoy** (Savoy Street) is the only relic of the Savoy Palace, although much restored by Queen Victoria after a fire in 1864. In the 1750s the Reverend John Wilkinson advertised to perform illegal marriages here. Today, many celebrities are legally wedded here, often attending a reception at the plush Savoy Hotel next door.

Savoy Theatre (Savoy Court) In 1881 Richard D'Oyly Carte built an extravagant new theatre on the site of the Savoy Palace for the production of operettas by the magical partnership of Gilbert and Sullivan. The Savoy theatre, the first public building in London to be illuminated by electricity, opened to the strains of *Patience,* soon followed by many other Gilbert and Sullivan successes. **Savoy Hotel** (Savoy Court) Built in 1889 adjacent to the Savoy Theatre, this luxurious hotel was also financed by Richard D'Oyly Carte. Today, the 300-bedroom Savoy, with its tucked-away entrance and quiet gardens surveying the Thames, is synonymous with comfort and wealth.

Somerset House (Lancaster Place), now occupied mainly by government offices including the Inland Revenue, stands on the site of a palace begun in 1547 by the Lord Protector Somerset, who five years later was to lose his head. The present building dates from 1785, its 180m southern façade originally rising sheer and magnificent out of the Thames with a distinctly Venetian aspect.

London's first hackney carriage rank stood outside the original St Mary-le-STRAND in the early-17thC. The present church, encircled by ceaseless traffic, was erected in 1714.

St Mary-le-STRAND Built on an island in the east end of the STRAND in 1714, this elegantly proportioned church won much praise for its architect, James Gibbs. Pevsner describes it enthusiastically as 'a casket one can handle with one's hands'. The present building replaced a much earlier one probably dating back to the 12thC. On a green in front of the church stood the famous **Maypole in the STRAND**, first erected in the 1500s. It was removed in 1718.

'What's not destroy'd by Time's devouring hand?
Where's Troy, and where's the Maypole in the STRAND?'
Revd James Bramston (c1694-1744) *Art of Politics*

St Clement Danes, on a more easterly island site that probably dates back to Danish times, was built by Sir Christopher Wren in 1680-2, although its graceful spire is another of James Gibbs's masterpieces. Immaculately restored following severe damage from enemy bombing in World War Two, this is now the central church for the Royal Air Force.

The **York Watergate** (Watergate Walk), at the end of Buckingham Street, once formed the gateway from the Duke of Buckingham's garden to his river steps. Built in 1626, and now marooned some 100m inland, it indicates clearly how much land was reclaimed from the Thames by the construction of the Victoria Embankment.

The **Victoria Embankment**, built between 1864-70, unified the frayed waterfront between Westminster and the City. Sir John Bazalgette's colossal granite and brick river-wall reclaimed from the Thames 15 ha of land and carried a broad new carriageway to relieve congestion on the STRAND. Entombed within it ran a new sewage system and the southern section of the underground railway's Inner Circle.

The York Watergate, looking downstream towards Somerset House, is seen here in its heyday when it led directly onto the river.

Number One the STRAND, which was the residence of the Secretary of State and next door to Northumberland House, was apparently, in the 1760s, the first house in London to be given an official street-number.

The **Halifax Building Society** (#51/55) is the London office of the world's largest building society. With total assets exceeding £29,000,000,000 the Halifax could comfortably finance saturation development on every building site of the MONOPOLY board.

James Boswell at the age of forty-five, painted in 1785 by the academician Sir Joshua Reynolds.

Famous people

James Boswell (1740-95), Scottish writer and libertine whose *Life of Samuel Johnson* has become an acknowledged classic, was no stranger to the STRAND. He augmented his string of temporary mistresses with many girls picked up here in the STRAND.

Sarah Siddons (1755-1831), the celebrated actress who made her first appearance at Drury Lane in 1775, lodged at #149 in 1782.

Samuel Taylor Coleridge (1772-1834), poet and philosopher, author of the magical *Ancient Mariner* and inspirational *Kubla Khan*, lodged for a time at #348.

George Eliot (1819-80), one of the greatest of English novelists whose real name was Mary Ann Evans, lived at #142 from 1851-5.

Richard D'Oyly Carte (1844-1901), who financed the Savoy Theatre and Hotel, was a flamboyant London musical-instrument maker turned impresario. By successfully promoting Gilbert and Sullivan's now famous comic operas, he amassed for himself a considerable fortune.

King Edward VII (1841-1910), when Prince of Wales, used to entertain the unconventional and stunningly beautiful actress **Lily Langtry** at the elegant 18thC restaurant started by Thomas Rule in Maiden Lane, just off the STRAND. To facilitate their clandestine arrival an entrance was built specifically for them.

Georgi Markov (d1978) In September 1978 the name of this otherwise obscure, exiled Bulgarian playwright, broadcasting for the BBC behind the Iron Curtain, suddenly became headline news. Victim of the Cold War, Markov had been bizarrely assassinated while strolling in the STRAND. Although the culprit has never been positively identified, it is almost certain that the murder weapon was a City umbrella – its tip containing a hypodermic needle loaded with ricin, a slow-acting, lethal poison extracted from castor-oil seeds.

Mark Thatcher, son of the British Prime Minister Margaret Thatcher, married Diane Burgdorf, daughter of Texan millionaire Ted Burgdorf, at the Savoy Chapel on St Valentine's Day 1987.

CHANCE

"DRUNK IN CHARGE" FINE £20

In which street, celebrated for its many pubs, used drunken drovers to amuse themselves by stampeding their cattle amongst the shops and market stalls?

a) OLD KENT ROAD

b) EUSTON ROAD

c) OXFORD STREET

YOU ARE ASSESSED FOR STREET REPAIRS £40 PER HOUSE £115 PER HOTEL

When was the Metropolitan Board of Works, London's first overall local authority, established?

a) 1347

b) 1605

c) 1855

PAY SCHOOL FEES OF £150

The London College of Music is at which of the following addresses?

a) Great MARLBOROUGH STREET

b) EUSTON ROAD

c) PICCADILLY

GO BACK THREE SPACES

Of all the streets on the Monopoly board, VINE STREET is:

a) furthest south

b) shortest and narrowest

c) oldest

MAKE GENERAL REPAIRS ON ALL OF YOUR HOUSES FOR EACH HOUSE PAY £25 FOR EACH HOTEL PAY £100

Who was the first 'speculative builder', the 'Emperor of the Building Trade'?

a) Lewis Cubitt

b) Thomas Cubitt

c) John Nash

answers: acabb

FLEET STREET

(EC4/City of London)

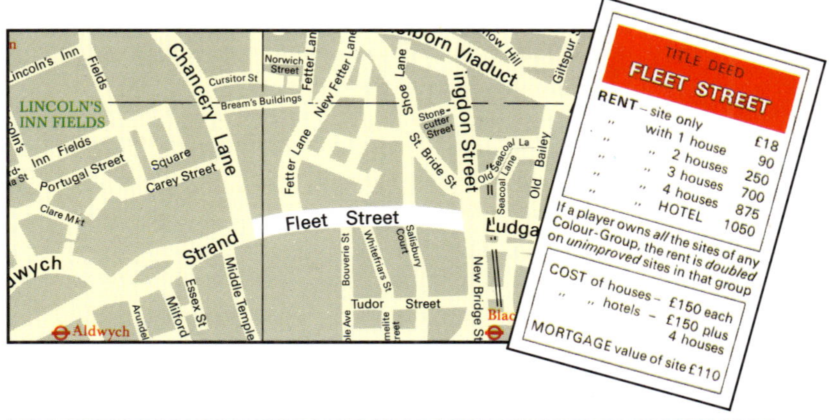

MONOPOLY valuation: £220

Current valuation: £195,000,000

Location description

'The man must have a rare recipe for melancholy, who can be dull in FLEET STREET.'

Charles Lamb (1775-1834)

***The Londoner* (in letter to Thomas Manning)**

FLEET STREET's 500m length probes eastwards from the STRAND into the City of London, soon dropping steeply to give spectacular views of St Paul's Cathedral. It is, in fact, the only MONOPOLY street to lie within the City walls. Its former army of journalists and printers, supplanted today by dealers in negotiable securities, have largely migrated eastwards; while the midnight throb of the printing presses for which it was once famed is but a thin echo in its narrow side streets.

Derivation of name

'Fleet', an Anglo-Saxon word meaning creek or tidal inlet, was originally applied to the lower reaches of the small river which flowed from Hampstead into the Thames west of Roman London. Eventually, this Fleet River, long since entombed beneath concrete and tarmacadam, gave its name to the street which climbed westwards up its sloping banks.

Short history

In Roman Londinium a road probably left the west wall of the City at the Lud Gate, just to the east of modern Ludgate Circus, crossing the River Fleet and taking roughly the course of modern FLEET STREET. By medieval times this route had been developed into an important thoroughfare, engulfed within the City's growing boundaries. FLEET STREET, as it was by then known, was lined with the houses of ecclesiastical dignitaries. Two ancient churches

This 16thC Agas map of London shows the Fleet River flowing into the Thames. Old St Paul's is seen on the right.

proclaimed the Christian gospel: St Dunstan's above, St Bride's below. And along its length royal processions would slowly wend from Westminster to the massive St Paul's Cathedral high up on Ludgate Hill.

It was not until the 16thC that FLEET STREET's traditional association with printing began. It originated not with Caxton, the first English printer, but with his foreman, Wynkyn de Worde. Under the sign of the Sun, on FLEET STREET's south side near today's Salisbury Court, de Worde set up shop with a hand-screw press in 1500. In the same year a Norman printer called Richard Pynson moved into FLEET STREET, opening a business at the other end near St Dunstan's church. In 1508 Pynson became official Printer to the King, publishing Henry VIII's famous denunciation of Martin Luther in 1521.

On Pynson's death in 1530 his royal appointment passed to another FLEET STREET pioneer of printing, Thomas Berthelet under the sign of Lucretia Romana. These early printers attracted to them everyone with an interest in the new technology. Thus it was to FLEET STREET that London printers, bookbinders, writers, publishers and booksellers gravitated in the 16thC, producing a spate of legal, ecclesiastical, educational and popular texts.

In 1702 came FLEET STREET's first newspaper, the *Daily Courant*. Launched by the printer Edward Mallet, 'next to the King's Arms Tavern by Fleet Bridge', it was taken over within one month by another printer, Samuel Buckley, 'at the Dolphin in Little Britain'. After that, national and provincial newspapers, press agencies and ancillary services proliferated in the 'street of ink'; and for two centuries and a half FLEET STREET became a synonym for journalism, its offices and taverns alive with the latest and most sensational stories. In the 1980s came the first serious reversal of this trend, as labour difficulties, computerization and soaring property values led some newspaper barons to seek discrete, more convenient production locations in London's disused dockland area to the east. Today, few papers are published here, but the great news agencies like Reuter's or the Press Association remain.

Numb. 7113.

The Daily Courant.

Thursday, March 25. 1725.

London, March 15.
Yesterday arrived the Mail from France.

Points of interest

Fleet River Rising in Hampstead, the modern Fleet flows under King's Cross and below Farringdon Road and Street, entering the Thames at Blackfriars. At first a defensive barrier to the west of Roman Londinium, it later became a minor waterway, conveying materials and people upstream, perhaps as far as King's Cross. By the 15thC it had become a public dump for refuse and sewage, eventually impassable for rivercraft. In 1733 its lower section was arched over. Today, encased in concrete, the Fleet River that gave its name to a world of journalism, forms part of London's sewage sytem.

Fleet Prison In this notorious, moated prison on the Fleet River's east bank, probably first erected soon after 1066, debtors and bankrupts traditionally languished. Yet those who fell foul of Henry VIII's Star Chamber and others also suffered here. In the mid-1500s the young Earl of Surrey, whose son built Northumberland House, was confined within these walls; in 1601 another poet, John Donne, was immured here for wedding Sir George More's daughter without his permission; and in 1708 William Penn, celebrated founder of Pennsylvania but now in debt, was thrown into the Fleet for nine months. Keepers of the Fleet grew rich by charging and overcharging their prisoners for food, 'accommodation' and privileges. Grimly described by Dickens in *Pickwick Papers*, the Fleet Prison was finally demolished in 1846.

John Donne (c1572-1631). His secret marriage to Anne More resulted in his imprisonment in the Fleet Prison.

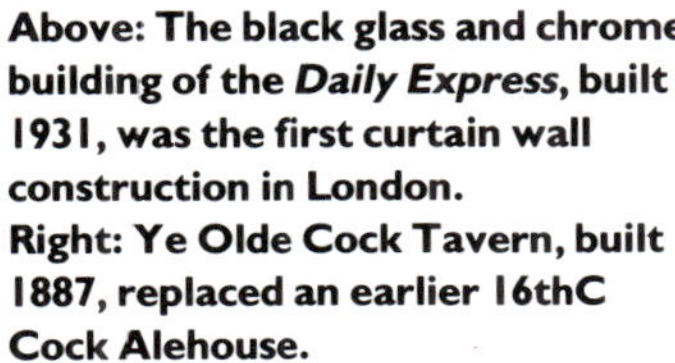
Above: The black glass and chrome building of the *Daily Express*, built 1931, was the first curtain wall construction in London.
Right: Ye Olde Cock Tavern, built 1887, replaced an earlier 16thC Cock Alehouse.

Fleet Marriages During the 17thC and early-18thC Fleet Prison was infamous for the clandestine marriages contracted without licence within its walls, the first notice of which was in 1613. Conducted mainly by clergymen who had themselves been imprisoned in the Fleet for debt, such espousals were outlawed by the Marriage Act of 1753.

Temple Bar At the junction of FLEET STREET and the STRAND, Temple Bar marked the western limits of the City of London. In the 13thC this function was performed by simple wooden posts and chain, later replaced by a stone gate with prison above. Rebuilt by Wren in 1670, Temple Bar was removed in 1877 to ease traffic congestion. In the 17thC and 18thC the heads and other extremities of traitors were often impaled on spikes set into its superstructure. In deference to the City's independence the monarch has always sought permission from the Lord Mayor before passing Temple Bar.

Temple In this exquisite legal quarter, with its strangely calm atmosphere and linked courtyards, lawyers have studied and worked for six centuries. Inner Temple and Middle Temple straddle much of the land between FLEET STREET and the Thames. In 1185 the Knights Templar, an influential order created to defend travellers in the Holy Land, consecrated a new temple on the banks of the Thames. Elegant cloisters connected the fine

Temple Church with a Hall of Priests and Hall of Knights. Yet the great wealth, privileges and immunities which the knights enjoyed won them enemies, leading eventually to their 14thC persecution and downfall. When most of their lands passed to the Knights Hospitaller, the Temple complex was leased to students and professors of the law who remain to this day.

Dr Johnson's House (#17 Gough Square) From the north side of FLEET STREET, Johnson's Court leads into Gough Square where, in the attic of this carefully preserved town-house, Dr Samuel Johnson and six clerks sweated over his *Dictionary* from 1747-55. In their elegant, late-17thC home Johnson's alcoholic wife Tetty died in bed from an overdose of opium in 1752.

Ye Olde Cheshire Cheese (Wine Office Court) To this ancient, oak-beamed pub, still popular with FLEET STREET journalists, came many men of letters including: Dr Johnson, Gibbon and Boswell; Charles Dickens, Forster and Thackeray; and Mark Twain, Yeats and Conan Doyle.

El Vino's (#47) Already well known as a preserve of newspapermen and lawyers, El Vino's wine bar shot to national fame in 1982 when the Court of Appeal ruled that it could no longer refuse service to women at its bar.

Dr Johnson's house in Gough Square is carefully preserved today.

Famous people

Wynkyn de Worde (d1535), who moved his flourishing printing and publishing business to FLEET STREET in 1500, was a pupil of Caxton. Unlike his more scholarly employer, who had produced classical books for a somewhat rarefied readership, de Worde was the first 'mass' publisher of popular works. Of the 800 books he produced, the last, *Complaint of the too soon maryed*, was published in the year of his death.

Dr Samuel Johnson (1709-84), lexicographer, writer and critic *par excellence* who lived for much of his life in and around FLEET STREET, was, despite great flair and boundless energy, beset by financial hardships until well into his fifties. In reply to Lord Chesterfield's 'kind' but belated commendation of his famous *Dictionary*, Johnson wrote stingingly that it had been 'delayed till I am indifferent and cannot enjoy it; till I am solitary and cannot impart it; till I am known and do not want it.'

Baron Paul Julius Reuter (1818-99), whose international news agency based at #85 is now a household word, was originally a telegraph promoter born at Cassel in Germany. In 1851 he transferred to London a successful organization that he had earlier formed at Aix-la-Chapelle for transmitting commercial news by telegraph. Reuter's today has nearly 3,000 employees across ninety countries.

Popular associations: Nelson's column / pigeons / New Year celebrations

TRAFALGAR SQUARE

(WC2, SW1/City of Westminster)

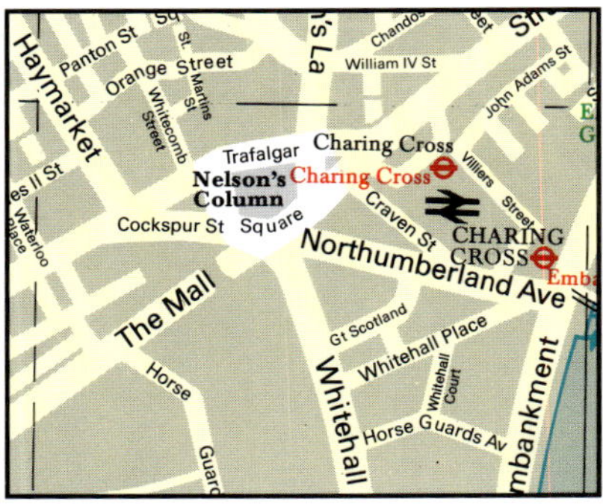

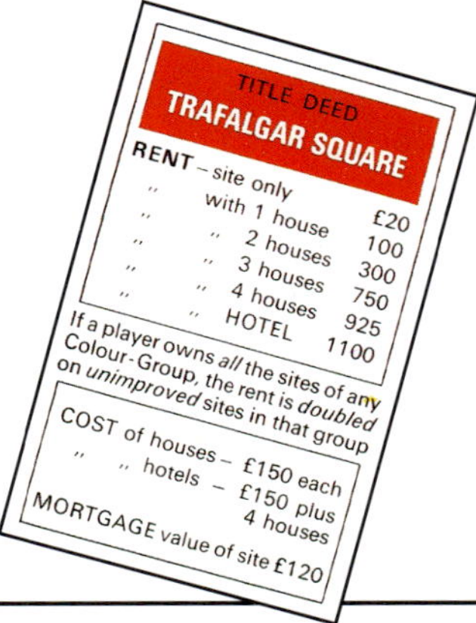

MONOPOLY valuation: £240

Current valuation: £115,500,000

Location description

Approximately 2.25ha in area, TRAFALGAR SQUARE is probably the most famous landmark on the MONOPOLY board. This pigeon-filled plaza, whose graceful plane trees and twin fountains cool four couchant bronze lions, is dominated by its imposing Nelson's Column. Uniting WHITEHALL with the STRAND, TRAFALGAR SQUARE forms one of the crucial junctions in the pattern of traditional London, the focal point of the metropolis to which all road distances are measured.

Derivation of name

Cape Trafalgar, on the south-west coast of Spain, was in 1805 the scene of an historic victory by the British fleet, commanded by Nelson, over the combined fleets of Spain and France. It was in commemoration of this battle that TRAFALGAR SQUARE was so named.

Short history

For hundreds of years the area at the northern end of WHITEHALL, now occupied by TRAFALGAR SQUARE, was used as a royal mews. Edward I's hawks were kept here and his falconers quartered here in the 13thC, when mew meant only a 'cage for hawks' and did not have the association with horses that it later acquired. Over the centuries the buildings were enlarged and stabling for the royal horses added. Burned down and rebuilt, they were also used in turn as lodgings, barracks, prison and public record office. Between the mews and WHITEHALL stood the Charing Cross, until destroyed in 1647.

By the 1820s the brilliant but ageing architect, John Nash, had won approval of his Charing Cross Improvement Scheme. He was not to live to see its fulfilment, but under it the royal mews were to be swept away and a wide, open plaza, later christened TRAFALGAR SQUARE, laid out. Work started in 1830. Over the next few decades the formal square was constructed, the National Gallery built to its north, Nelson's Column erected and its lions positioned, and two granite fountains and basins installed. Since then a few minor alterations have been made, NORTHUMBERLAND AVENUE opposite has been opened up, and Admiralty Arch and various statues added; but the square nevertheless retains the openness of its original concept.

Almost since its beginnings, TRAFALGAR SQUARE has been a magnet for crowds attending social and political rallies, as well as an annual venue for colourful and spirited New Year celebrations.

Left: The colonnaded National Gallery rises just beyond TRAFALGAR SQUARE's north terrace.
Above: In 1873 the lions at the foot of Nelson's Column were decorated with mourning wreaths on the death of their creator, Sir Edwin Henry Landseer.

Points of interest

Charing Cross The original Charing Cross was erected in 1291 by Edward I to mark the last stage of his wife's funeral procession from Nottinghamshire to Westminster Abbey. It stood at the small hamlet of Charing, today the junction of WHITEHALL and TRAFALGAR SQUARE, on the spot where the equestrian statue of Charles I now stands. The original cross was demolished in 1647, but a replica, built in 1865 at a cost of £1,800, still adorns the forecourt of nearby Charing Cross Station.

Shortly before Nelson's statue was hauled up in 1843, fourteen stonemasons held a traditional topping-out celebration by dining at the summit of its 51m column.

Nelson's Column Perched on top of the 51m Corinthian column is a 5.3m high stone statue of Nelson erected to commemorate his great victory at Trafalgar. The Devonshire granite column was by William Railton, winner of a competition for its design. Nelson's sixteen tonne statue, hauled up in 1843, was sculpted by Edward Bailey. At the base of the column are four poignant bronze bas-reliefs, cast from captured French cannon, depicting: the Battle of Cape St Vincent; the Battle of the Nile; the bombardment of Copenhagen; and the death of Nelson. Around the column's pedestal lie Sir Edwin Landseer's four colossal bronze lions, heads raised and alert to guard the approaches to the fluted column towering overhead. The two neighbouring ornamental granite fountains, floodlit by night and originally placed here in 1845, were completely redesigned in 1939 by Sir Edwin Lutyens.

Below: The fountain pools of TRAFALGAR SQUARE are lined with blue tiles and decorated with bronze dolphins, mermaids and mermen.
Right: Norway's annual Christmas Tree gift is traditionally 30cm (one foot) longer each year.

Norwegian Christmas tree Every December the people of Norway donate to the people of Britain a massive fir tree in gratitude for the hospitality extended to their royal family during the Second World War. Set up in TRAFALGAR SQUARE and spectacularly illuminated, it yearly becomes the focal point of carol-singing and Christmas celebrations.

National Gallery Built in 1832-8 along the north side of TRAFALGAR SQUARE, the National Gallery is unquestionably one of the world's premier collections of art. It was born out of thirty-eight pictures which the British Government were reluctantly persuaded to redeem from the estate of the Russian-born John Julius Angerstein, thus forming the beginnings of a national collection and preventing them going to William of Orange.

TRAFALGAR SQUARE Police Station Hidden within a sturdy granite lamp-post in the south-east corner of the square is the smallest 'police station' in Britain, just large enough for one policeman. Erected in the late-19thC as a secret observation post with arrow-slit windows from which to monitor political meetings, the outpost had a direct telephone link to Cannon Row Police Station.

British Standard Measurements At the centre of TRAFALGAR SQUARE's north wall the standard imperial measures of inch, foot and yard are set out in metal; while on the east side of the square a plaque marks the official centre of London, to which all distances on signposts are measured.

Famous people

Edward I (1239-1307), King of England whose memorial to his wife lives on in the name of Charing Cross, was born at Westminster. An accomplished warrior, in 1254 he married Eleanor of Castile who travelled with him on the Crusades, probably saving his life by sucking poison from a wound. Eleanor died in 1290 and one tradition suggests that the name Charing derived from 'chère reine' in reference to Edward's 'dear queen'.

Viscount Horatio Nelson (1758-1805), dramatic centrepiece of TRAFALGAR SQUARE, was a brilliant naval commander who rose to heroic status from humble origins. In 1794 a piece of debris, thrown up by a shot, destroyed his right eye; three years later, by now rear-admiral, his right arm was badly wounded and subsequently amputated. In 1805 Nelson sailed to the southern Spanish seas, appearing off Cadiz on 29 September and blockading the French fleet, thus thwarting Napoleon's plan for the invasion of Britain. On 20 October the French admiral, Villeneuve, put to sea. To Nelson's twenty-seven ships-of-the-line, the combined French and Spanish forces numbered thirty-three. This was the scene for Nelson's historic signal: 'England expects every man this day to do his duty.' In the ensuing battle the *Redoubtable* and Nelson's *Victory* became locked with the enemy *Teméraire* and *Fougeux,* forming 'as compact a tier as if they had been moored together'. From a mast of the *Redoubtable* a stray musket-shot rang out that pierced the epaulet of Nelson's left shoulder and lodged in his back. Three hours later Viscount Nelson lay dead below-decks and the French and Spanish fleets had been annihilated. This decisive victory saved Britain from all danger of invasion and led ultimately to the liberation of Europe from Napoleon's dictatorial grip.

Sir Edwin Henry Landseer (1802-73), who modelled the bronze lions at the foot of Nelson's Column, was a celebrated animal painter who had exhibited at the Royal Academy at the early age of thirteen. Although his favourite and most successful subjects were dogs and deer, his gentle TRAFALGAR SQUARE lions are masterpieces of animal study, invariably popular with children and adults alike.

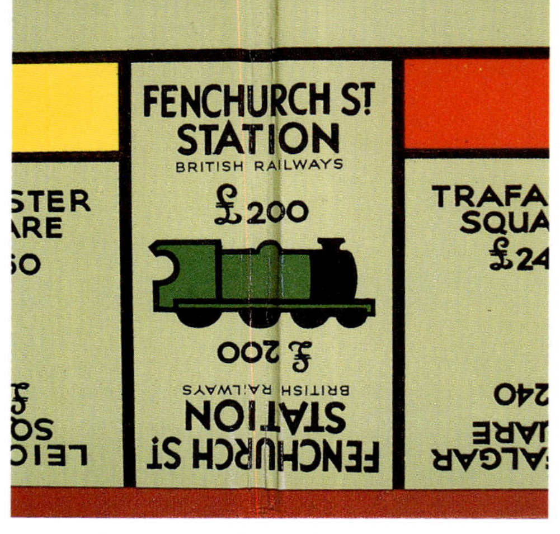

FENCHURCH S^T STATION

(Railway Place, EC3/City of London)

A small but busy City terminus for British Rail's Eastern Region, FENCHURCH STREET STATION is the most easterly on the MONOPOLY board.

MONOPOLY valuation: £200

Current valuation: £320,000,000

Opening date:

1841

Principal destinations

Include Basildon, Southend, Tilbury

Traffic statistics

Passenger trains daily: 280

Passengers daily: 64,000

Station background

On 2 August 1841, when little FENCHURCH STREET STATION opened for business, none of the other three termini on the MONOPOLY board existed. Noble KING'S CROSS STATION was more than ten and giant LIVERPOOL STREET STATION more than twenty years away: while exotic MARYLEBONE STATION would not be built until the turn of the century. FENCHURCH STREET STATION was in fact only the seventh terminus in London, and the first to penetrate the City.

The revolutionary new railways of the early/mid-19thC challenged the ascendancy of water-borne travel. River traffic on the Thames was at its peak, passengers for the Continent embarking downstream from London Bridge and sailing eastwards around the lengthy, horseshoe bend of the Isle of Dogs before stopping off at Blackwall. Directors of the London and Blackwall Railway perceived that a short 6km rail link from the City to Blackwall would offer river passengers a valuable short cut and at the same time connect the vast Thames-side dock complex with the commercial capital. Their first terminus, at the Minories – just outside the City boundary – was almost immediately superseded by FENCHURCH STREET STATION when permission was granted to carry the line right into the City, just south of the ancient thoroughfare of Fenchurch Street. A viaduct conveyed the track through this heavily congested area. To avoid all risk of fire started by steam trains in a built-up district, the carriages were pulled along by endless wire ropes driven by great stationary engines at Blackwall and the Minories. From the Minories to FENCHURCH STREET STATION no cable existed, and trains had to coast up the gentle 0.4km incline under their own impetus, departing from the terminus by gravity after being given 'only a slight push from the platform staff'. Gradually this isolated railway, which never in fact achieved great success, was linked to the lines of other companies and thus into a wider network.

Today, sited on choice City land, little FENCHURCH STREET STATION has been imaginatively redeveloped, a pyramid of crystal offices shimmering above it. Its original maritime flavour is no more. Tucked away in Railway Place, it is the least known and most compact terminus in London. No scent of romance hangs on its commercial air. No great express trains thunder through the night to alight at its four modest platforms. Its uttermost destination is a mere 65km away. Yet FENCHURCH STREET STATION disgorges more passengers daily than KING'S CROSS STATION and MARYLEBONE STATION combined, processing nearly half of these in the peak hours between 7 and 10am.

Left: In 1983 approval was granted for a £28 million redevelopment scheme under which FENCHURCH STREET STATION's listed frontage would be retained and restored. Right: At its two island platforms – each with two working faces – 29,000 City-bound passengers daily alight between 7 and 10am.

The office pyramid surmounting the original FENCHURCH STREET STATION façade was funded by the Norwich Union Insurance Group.

Station timetable

1836: permission received for 5.6km line between Blackwall and the Minories.

1839: permission received for 0.4km extension and construction of new terminus at Fenchurch Street.

1841 (2 August): FENCHURCH STREET STATION opens.

1849: steam locomotives replace cable traction.

1849: new branch line to Eastern Counties Railway.

1850: line gains access to Islington and beyond.

1853: Minories Station closes.

1854: FENCHURCH STREET STATION enlarged and modernised. New connection to Tilbury.

1881: fast business service to Southend commences.

1908: Sunday trains to Blackwall discontinued.

1926: Blackwall service suspended through General Strike and finally abandoned.

1932-35: FENCHURCH STREET STATION undergoes major modernisation scheme. Now 70,000 passengers daily.

1949: FENCHURCH STREET STATION joins Eastern Region.

1962: fully accelerated electric train service initiated. Steam passenger trains withdrawn.

1984: work starts on £28 million redevelopment scheme, including 8,700m^2 air-conditioned offices.

1987: completion of pyramid construction offices mounted over restored, original station façade.

Popular associations: Cinema / mass entertainment / gateway to Chinatown

LEICESTER SQUARE

(WC2/City of Westminster)

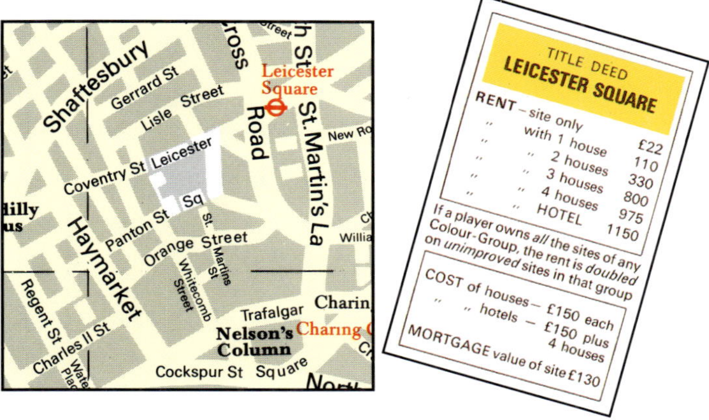

MONOPOLY valuation: £260
Current valuation: £36,000,000

Location description

300m east of PICCADILLY Circus and linked to it by COVENTRY STREET, LEICESTER SQUARE is at the very heart of London's screenland. Once fashionable and strictly residential, it is today a quaint and leafy oasis of pedestrian calm flanked by cinemas, theatres, restaurants and amusement arcades dedicated to a world of mass entertainment.

Derivation of name

LEICESTER SQUARE derives its name from the earls of Leicester, whose town house stood here in the 17thC and 18thC.

Short history

In the late 1530s Henry VIII acquired 3 hectares of land known as St Martin's Field just north of the Royal Mews at Charing Cross. Part of this he had confiscated from the Abbott and Convent of St Peter's, Westminster Abbey; and part secured from the Beaumont family. Mid-16thC maps depict it as open Lammas land. Here, following the Lammas festival which celebrated the harvesting of the crops, commoners could graze their livestock and lay out their washing. Then in 1630 and again in 1648 Robert Sidney, 2nd Earl of Leicester, bought parcels of this land. On the northern part of his new estate the earl erected, in 1631-5, a vast and attractive mansion which he named Leicester House.

Gradually the area to the south of Leicester House became known as Leicester Fields. Because this was still Lammas land the earl was required to compensate the parish for the loss of grazing rights and to convert the field into walks planted with trees, with 'spaces left for the Inhabitantes to drye their clothes there as they were wont, and to have free use of the place.'

When, in 1670, its three remaining sides were tastefully developed as LEICESTER SQUARE, the central area was fenced off to form a garden. The newly built, elegant town houses with their distinguished residents soon acquired a fashionable status; but the garden, passing through several new owners, suffered badly from neglect.

At last, in 1874, LEICESTER SQUARE's garden was bought for over £11,000 by the fake Baron Grant who restored it with the help of the architect, Sir James Knowles. At the centre he planted a marble statue of William Shakespeare by Giovanni Fontana ('unpretentious' is how Pevsner describes it); at each corner the bust of one great resident of the square ('bedraggled'); and between them the majestic plane trees whose green leaves today dapple the surrounding lawns and tulip-beds. On its completion Grant flamboyantly presented it to the nation.

By this time the residential flavour of LEICESTER SQUARE had gone forever. Leicester House had been demolished in 1792. The construction of New COVENTRY STREET c1845 across the square's northern edge had brought a vulgar traffic, shattering the enclave's former calm. Shops, exhibition halls, even foreign hotels and Turkish baths, sprang up on all sides; yet it was for its late-Victorian music-halls and attendant *filles de joie* that LEICESTER SQUARE became known pre-eminently as a world of masculine distraction and dissipation. And it was to this carefree world that the nostalgic First World War song, 'It's a Long Way to Tipperary', bade such a prophetic 'Farewell, LEICESTER SQUARE'.

LEICESTER SQUARE in 1753. 'This Perspective View of the South West Prospect is most Humbly Inscrib'd to his Royal Highness the Prince of Wales by his most obedient humble servant to command – John Brindley.' Note the Sedan chairs which survived well into the 19thC.

Duels of honour and revenge were once fought where tulip beds now embellish a springtime LEICESTER SQUARE.

Points of interest

Leicester House, built on land effectively bounded by the present Leicester Street, Lisle Street, Leicester Place and New COVENTRY STREET, was one of the largest mansions in 17thC London. Famous for its hospitality, its many prominent guests were frequently amused by hired entertainers. In 1717 the future George II moved in as Prince of Wales following a squabble with his father. In 1741 his son, Frederick Prince of Wales, did the same. Thus it was that Thomas Pennant described Leicester House as the 'pouting-place of princes'.

Empire Theatre/ Cinema The Empire Theatre, opened in 1884 on the north side of LEICESTER SQUARE, was converted from the unsuccessful Royal London Panorama theatre erected only three years before; but it, too, did not attract capacity audiences until it reopened as a music-hall in 1887. In 1894, at the instigation of a Mrs Ormiston Chant, screens were installed to separate the theatre's bars from its notorious adjoining promenade, where good-looking and amiable women of the town used to display themselves. The fury that these thin canvas screens aroused was tempestuous, raging for weeks in correspondence to the press. On 3 November, the Saturday after their installation, a young Sandhurst cadet named Winston Churchill led a mob of several hundred in demolishing them. But the 'prowling of the prudes', as Churchill described it, was to prevail. Today the Empire is a civilized cinema with two screens of another kind.

The garish lights of 20thC entertainment – for which **LEICESTER SQUARE** is a modern metaphor – blend bizzarely with traditional architecture.

Charlie Chaplin In early 1981, more than a hundred years after Baron Grant had erected his monument to William Shakespeare, Sir Ralph Richardson unveiled a bronze statue of that virtuoso of entertainers, Charlie Chaplin. Sculpted by John Doubleday, it depicts the legendary master of the silver screen in his customary bowler hat, with the caption: 'The comic genius who gave pleasure to so many.'

Beefsteak Club (#9 Irving Street) The original Sublime Society of Beef-Steaks, whose distinguished members had met weekly for a beef-steak dinner since 1735, was dissolved in 1867. Nine years later the Beefsteak Club resurrected the name and in 1896 moved to its present venue over a shop just off LEICESTER SQUARE. Its mixed and eminent membership of authors, actors, politicians and academics are obliged by its rules to talk to one another. The steward and waiters who serve them beefsteak dinners at the long table are all known as 'Charles' – regardless of their real names.

Old Curiosity Shop (#10 Irving Street) The address next to the Beefsteak Society is traditionally the home of Little Nell, heroine of Charles Dickens's *Old Curiosity Shop* serialised in 1841. The story of the tragic Nell, forced to flee from her home by the malevolent Mr Quilp, conquered the world. Mail-boats docking in far-flung ports were met by waiting crowds, desperate for news of Little Nell's plight.

Famous people

William Hogarth (1697-1764), sensitive English painter and engraver, was a native of London who died in LEICESTER SQUARE after occupying #30 from 1733. Four years before moving here he had eloped with and married the daughter of his tutor, Sir James Thornhill. At LEICESTER SQUARE Hogarth created many of his impossibly crowded canvases, grim social commentaries and savage political caricatures, including the *Rake's Progress, Industry and Idleness* and the *Four Stages of Cruelty*.

Sir Joshua Reynolds (1723-92), star of the English school of portraiture and author of some 2,500 paintings, lived from 1760 at #47, later built over by the headquarters of the Automobile Association, Fanum House. Born near Plymouth the seventh son of a clergyman, his fame and fortune seemed to know no bounds. In 1764, together with the apparently omnipresent Dr Johnson, he founded the exclusive, almost incestuous, Literary Club. In 1768 he was elected the first president of the illustrious Royal Academy, and in the following year he was knighted. Johnson wrote with envy of his great wealth. Yet one story tells of a poverty-stricken young model sitting on the steps of #47, in tears because Reynolds had refused to exchange the bad shilling with which he had paid her.

Sir Joshua Reynolds – exotic self-portrait of c1747.

Baron Grant (1830-99), rescuer of the LEICESTER SQUARE garden when virtual wasteland, was born in Dublin under the name Gottheimer. He soon acquired a dubious fortune by becoming a 'pioneer of modern mammoth company promoting'. Twice Member of Parliament for Kidderminster, he changed his name from Gottheimer to the more Anglo-Saxon sounding Grant. This he later elaborated with the title 'Baron'. Shortly after his flamboyant presentation of the garden to 'the people of London', Grant was ignominiously exposed for fraud. Subsequently bankrupted, the Baron died in comparative poverty.

Popular associations: Entertainment/eating-places

COVENTRY STREET

(W1/City of Westminster)

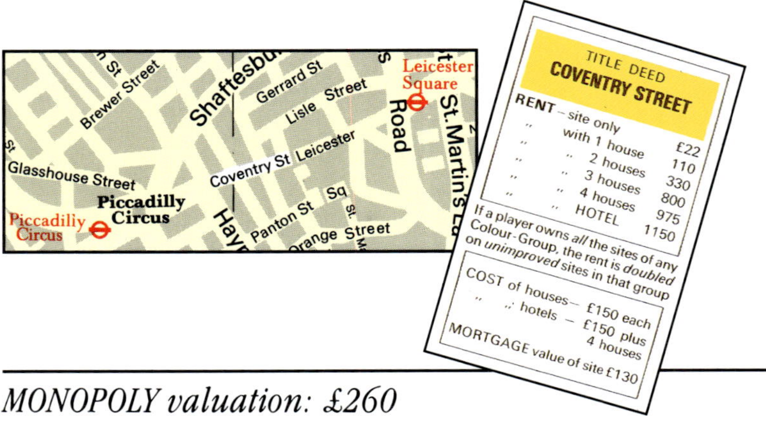

MONOPOLY valuation: £260

Current valuation: £75,000,000

Location description

A busy 250m thoroughfare thronged with faces of all nationalities, COVENTRY STREET prolongs PICCADILLY eastwards towards LEICESTER SQUARE. Once notorious for its gaming-houses, modern COVENTRY STREET is a cosmopolitan medley of small shops, bureaux-de-change, eating places, amusement arcades, dance halls, cinemas and theatres.

Derivation of name

COVENTRY STREET took its name from Charles II's Secretary of State, Henry Coventry, who lived in the adjoining Shaver's Place or Coventry Court.

Short history

Laid out early in the 1680s, COVENTRY STREET linked the then newly developed PICCADILLY to the equally new Whitcomb Street at a time when this part of London was undergoing major development. It was never really a residential street, its numerous gaming-tables soon acquiring for it a dubious reputation as a place of entertainment. In 1814 COVENTRY STREET was, together with PICCADILLY, the first street in London to have gas lighting permanently installed.

New COVENTRY STREET, extending COVENTRY STREET eastwards across the north side of LEICESTER SQUARE to Cranbourne Street, was built c1845 to relieve traffic congestion in the area.

Points of interest

The **Trocadero** The original Trocadero Palace – popularly the 'Troc' – was a music-hall at the junction of Great Windmill Street and COVENTRY STREET at the end of the 19thC. In 1984 a new Trocadero complex opened as a spacious, seven-days-a-week shopping centre equipped with restaurant and entertainment facilities. Among its attractions are the Guinness World of Records, an imaginative exhibition of the *Guinness Book of Records,* and the

London Experience, a lavish, multi-screen, audio-visual history of London. Next door, reconstruction behind its existing façade is converting the London Pavilion, a famous landmark music-hall built in 1886, into a lavish new retail and leisure complex.

The **Prince of Wales Theatre** on the south side of COVENTRY STREET, dating back to 1884 when it was called the Prince's Theatre, is best known for its revues, musicals and farces.

Sandwiched between PICCADILLY and LEICESTER SQUARE, COVENTRY STREET is at the very heart of London.

Shaver's Place, which forms a right-angle between Haymarket and COVENTRY STREET, was the site of the 17thC Shaver's Hall, a notorious gaming-house run by Simon Osbaldeston, prosperous former barber to the Lord Chamberlain. In Shaver's Hall, Osbaldeston's gambling clientele were given a closer shave than was good for their wealth. He had acquired the town house previously built by Henry, Earl of Coventry, who had given his name to COVENTRY STREET. 18thC maps show this street, but describe it as 'Coventry Court'.

The **Café de Paris (#3)**, opposite the Prince of Wales Theatre, was converted from the pre-First World War basement of the Rialto Cinema. In the 1930s the Café de Paris was an exclusive night-club haunted by the flower of London society, later becoming one of London's best-known ballrooms. But the Second World War was to bring tragedy. At 9:45 on the night of 8 March 1941, German bombers loosed two 50kg landmines which careered through the Rialto cinema above and exploded on the densely-packed Saturday night dance-floor. Over seventy were killed instantly. Among the dead were the band-leader, Ken 'Snakehips' Johnson, and many of his band.

Henry Coventry gave his name first to Coventry Court and then to COVENTRY STREET.

Famous people

The **Duke of Windsor** (1894-1972), briefly Edward VIII before his abdication, was, with Mrs Simpson, among the inter-war glitterati to patronise the Café de Paris in COVENTRY STREET. **David Niven**, popular film-star, producer and best-selling author, met his first wife, Primula, at the Café de Paris. Other world famous guests have included the **Prince Aga Khan, Princess Margaret, Vivien Leigh, Sophia Loren, Tyrone Power, Jimmy Savile** and **Elizabeth Taylor.**

Vivien Leigh by Sasha, taken in 1937 when the Café de Paris that she patronised was at the height of its fame. Two years later Vivien Leigh was to achieve international stardom with the rôle of Scarlet O'Hara in *Gone With the Wind.*

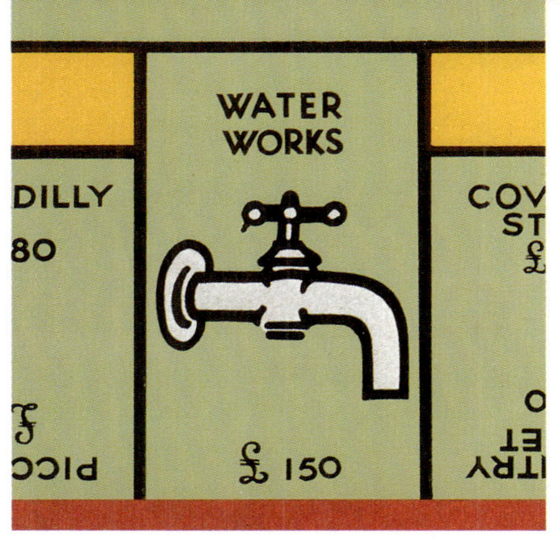

WATER WORKS

MONOPOLY valuation: £150
Current valuation: £1,000,000,000

It was the Thames that gave birth to London; and it is the Thames that sustains it today. The demand for water in the metropolis is unremitting. Water gushes from the ceaseless fountains of TRAFALGAR SQUARE; it bathes the industrious residents of the OLD KENT ROAD and purifies the smart streets of MAYFAIR; it irrigates the savoury kitchens of PARK LANE, grooms the immaculate horses of WHITEHALL and nourishes the green gardens of LEICESTER SQUARE. This priceless commodity – fifty percent of which is derived from the Thames – must be garnered and warehoused, cleansed, distributed and dispensed without fail twenty-four hours a day.

The Thames Water Authority is MONOPOLY London's WATER WORKS – one of the world's largest water undertakings. Through 30,000km of subterranean water mains its 9,000 staff supply up to 5,000,000,000 litres of water per day to some 11,000,000 people – 7,000,000 of whom live and work in the London area. Allowing for 20,000,000 tourists supplied annually by Thames Water, the average daily consumption per person is estimated at 160 litres.

Yet Thames Water's responsibilities also include the disposal of sewage; control of river pollution; rearing of fish; maintenance of river quality along some 2,600km of waterway; drainage of land and prevention of flooding; and the operation of the 'Eighth Wonder of the World' – the Thames Barrier completed in 1982 as part of a flood defence scheme for the whole of London.

The 520m Thames Barrier at Woolwich Reach is the world's largest movable flood barrier – ten massive steel gates pivoting electro-hydraulically between titanic piers and sills formed from 500,000 tonnes of concrete. When closed, each of its four main shipping gates rises as high as a five-storey building and weighs over 3,500 tonnes – heavier than a naval destroyer.

Popular associations: Select shops / exclusive hotels

PICCADILLY

(W1/City of Westminster)

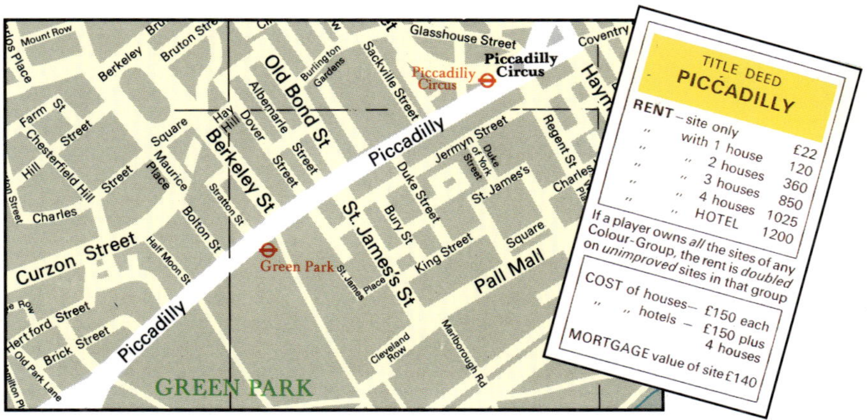

MONOPOLY valuation: £280
Current valuation: £526,800,000

Location description

A broad, distinguished avenue with an air of prosperity, modern PICCADILLY extends from Hyde Park Corner in the west to COVENTRY STREET in the east. North lies MAYFAIR; south lie Green Park and the district of St James's. Along its 1.3km length may be found the offices of international airlines, exclusive car showrooms, glamorous hotels, seductive arcades and prestigious shops. At its junction with COVENTRY STREET, REGENT STREET and Shaftesbury Avenue a statue of Eros adorns the famous once hub-of-Empire, PICCADILLY Circus.

Derivation of name

PICCADILLY's improbable name derives from the former, nearby Pickadilly Hall, home of a wealthy 17thC draper who made a fortune selling fashionable 'pickadils' (delicate frillings on collars or hems) to an aristocratic clientele.

Short history

For hundreds of years westward-bound travellers took either of two timeworn routes out of London. The 16thC Agas map depicts them as 'The Waye to Vxbridge' (modern OXFORD STREET) and 'The Waye to Redinge' (modern PICCADILLY). In those days this section of the Reading road was a leafy country lane, whose hedgerows overlooked grazing livestock and rich pastures. Two centuries later it had been overtaken by an exploding City of Westminster.

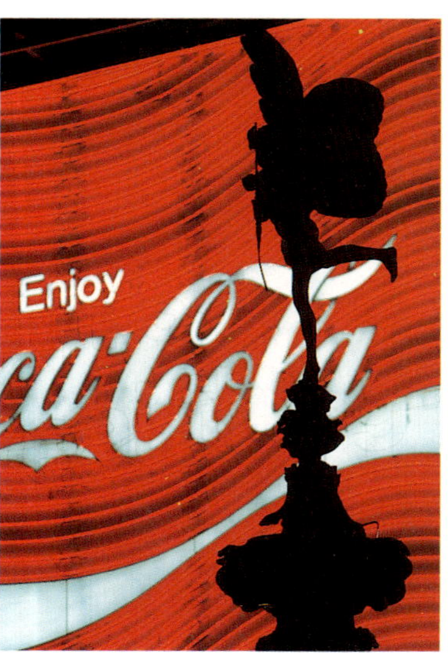

Left: The ground floor of Fortnum & Mason is the preserve of grocery. Above are displayed perfumes and fashion.
Right: Eros's arrow, aimed at the ground, is purportedly a play on the name of Lord Shaftesbury in memory of whom the monument was erected.

In 1612 the draper Robert Baker invested his new-found wealth in open land just north of modern-day PICCADILLY Circus. On it he built himself a baronial country mansion which local people immediately dubbed Pickadilly Hall, probably in mock reference to the fashionable pickadils which had made him wealthy. It was a good joke, and it stuck – not only to the house but to the local section of the passing Reading road.

Still, the road itself was not built-up. Only after the Civil War and the Restoration of Charles II in 1660 did widespread development begin. A prestigious and much sought after residential address, it was officially designated Portugal Street in deference to the king's new Portuguese wife, Catherine of Braganza. Yet, as with the attempt similarly to honour the unfortunate queen by calling PALL MALL Catherine Street, the popular name prevailed; and as construction progressed westward the nickname 'Pickadilly' accompanied it, gradually acquiring the modern spelling and achieving official status.

Points of interest

Shopping The quintessentially English stores of PICCADILLY seem to perpetuate its sweet air of success. In its alluring PICCADILLY Arcade built in 1910, brilliantly-lit arrays of exotic gifts gleam through dazzling plate-glass. The name of Fortnum and Mason (#181), luxurious royal provision merchants of the mid-18thC, is still whispered in state-rooms the world. Hatchard's (#187), another 18thC name, is synonymous with books and good literature. Simpson's (#203), a later 20thC arrival, is home of elegant fashion and sportswear.

PICCADILLY Circus When John Nash laid out REGENT STREET in the early-19thC, linking the Prince Regent's official residence at Carlton House with his new summer palace in Regent's Park, the Regent himself was anxious to prevent 'the sensation of crossing PICCADILLY'. To cater for this royal whim, Nash created a graceful, circular *place* at the intersection of the new Regent Street with PICCADILLY. Regent Circus, as this intimate crossing was named, came to be called PICCADILLY Circus in the 1880s when the symmetry of Nash's arrangement was destroyed by the creation of Shaftesbury Avenue. In 1893 the aluminium statue which made PICCADILLY Circus the 'meeting-place of the world' was unveiled. **Eros**, erected in memory of the philanthropic Lord Shaftesbury and fashioned by a young Albert Gilbert, was intended to represent the Angel of Christian Charity rather than the Greek God of Love.

The Ritz Hotel Midway along PICCADILLY's southern side, the Norwegian-granite and Portland-stone façade of the stylish Ritz Hotel forms a spacious arcade for pedestrians. Built in 1904-06 by the Swiss hotelier César Ritz, whose Paris Ritz was already a success, this was one of the first steel-framed buildings in London. The Ritz, with its sumptuous Louis XVI-style interior, crystal chandeliers and impeccable service, is a magical PICCADILLY landmark that glistens spectacularly at night.

The pedestrian arcade beneath the Ritz Hotel is one of the features of modern Picadilly.

Royal Academy of Arts (Burlington House) First presided over in 1768 by the LEICESTER SQUARE luminary Sir Joshua Reynolds, the Royal Academy was founded with the aim of fostering British art. Exactly one hundred years later, the Academy moved to its present location in what had been the classically proportioned 17thC and 18thC mansion of the Earls of Burlington. Today, the Academy is most famous for its annual Summer Exhibition which marks the start of the London season.

Famous people

Lord Byron (1788-1824), noble poet whose fantasy *Childe Harold* made him an overnight success at the age of twenty-four, lived at #139 as the lion of London. His poetic prowess and political pursuits carried him to a social pinnacle from which he was shortly to plummet, brutally ostracized for a more than brotherly interest in his half-sister, Augusta Leigh.

Mrs Porter, the notorious 19thC procuress, maintained a high-class bordello on the north side of PICCADILLY in Berkeley Street. Through Mrs Porter, the Duke of Wellington became entangled with the mean-lipped courtesan Harriette Wilson, whose blackmailing threats to reveal all in her *Memoirs* of 1825 led to the Iron Duke's legendary remark: 'Publish and be damned!'

Sir Alfred Gilbert (1854-1934), creator of Eros, was a young, idealistic and successful London-born sculptor when commissioned to create a memorial to the factory reformer, Lord Shaftesbury. Within a few years the statue he created had embarrassed him publically and crippled him financially, forcing him to retire to Belgium. With the high cost of bronze the memorial had cost Gilbert £7,000: for it he was paid £3,000. Interference by the memorial committee had seriously compromised Gilbert's inspired design; and its brazen and impudent nakedness at the hub-of-Empire was too much for the squeamish. Yet by the time Gilbert returned to England in 1932 to receive an overdue knighthood, the British public had taken Eros to their hearts.

Lord Peter Wimsey, the aristocratic detective launched on the world in 1923 by advertising copywriter Dorothy L Sayers, occupied #110a for many years. Perhaps Lord Peter's most consummate investigations were those of *Murder Must Advertise* (1933) and *The Nine Tailors* .

George VI (1895-1952), who became King of England on the abdication of his elder brother Edward VIII in 1936, resided for a time as Duke of York at #145.

CHANCE
LIVERPOOL ST. STATION BRITISH RAILWAYS £200
PARK LANE £350
COMMUNITY
GET OUT OF JA
SUPER TAX PAY £100
MAYFAIR £400
OLD KENT ROAD £60
COLLECT £200 SALARY AS YOU PASS
GO
MONOPOLY
500
KING'S CROSS STATION
BRITISH RAILWAYS
RENT £25
If 2 stations are owned 50
If 3 " " " 100
If 4 " " " 200
MORTGAGE value — £100
TITLE DEED
BOND STREET
RENT – site only £28
with 1 house 150
" 2 houses 450
" 3 houses 1000
" 4 houses 1200
HOTEL 1400

SIDE 4

GO TO JAIL ➧ MAYFAIR

Where petty thieves once rode to hang on the communal Tyburn gallows tourists now throng a busy OXFORD STREET – one of Side 4's three green shopping thoroughfares. With its vast, City-based LIVERPOOL STREET STATION and exclusive West End locations, the current valuation of Side 4 far exceeds that of the rest of the board. MAYFAIR is the ultimate square. Here resides all that is most glamorous and opulent in MONOPOLY London – a repository of the rich and famous for whom 'High Street' means nearby BOND STREET and 'pied-à-terre' *a penthouse suite in PARK LANE.*

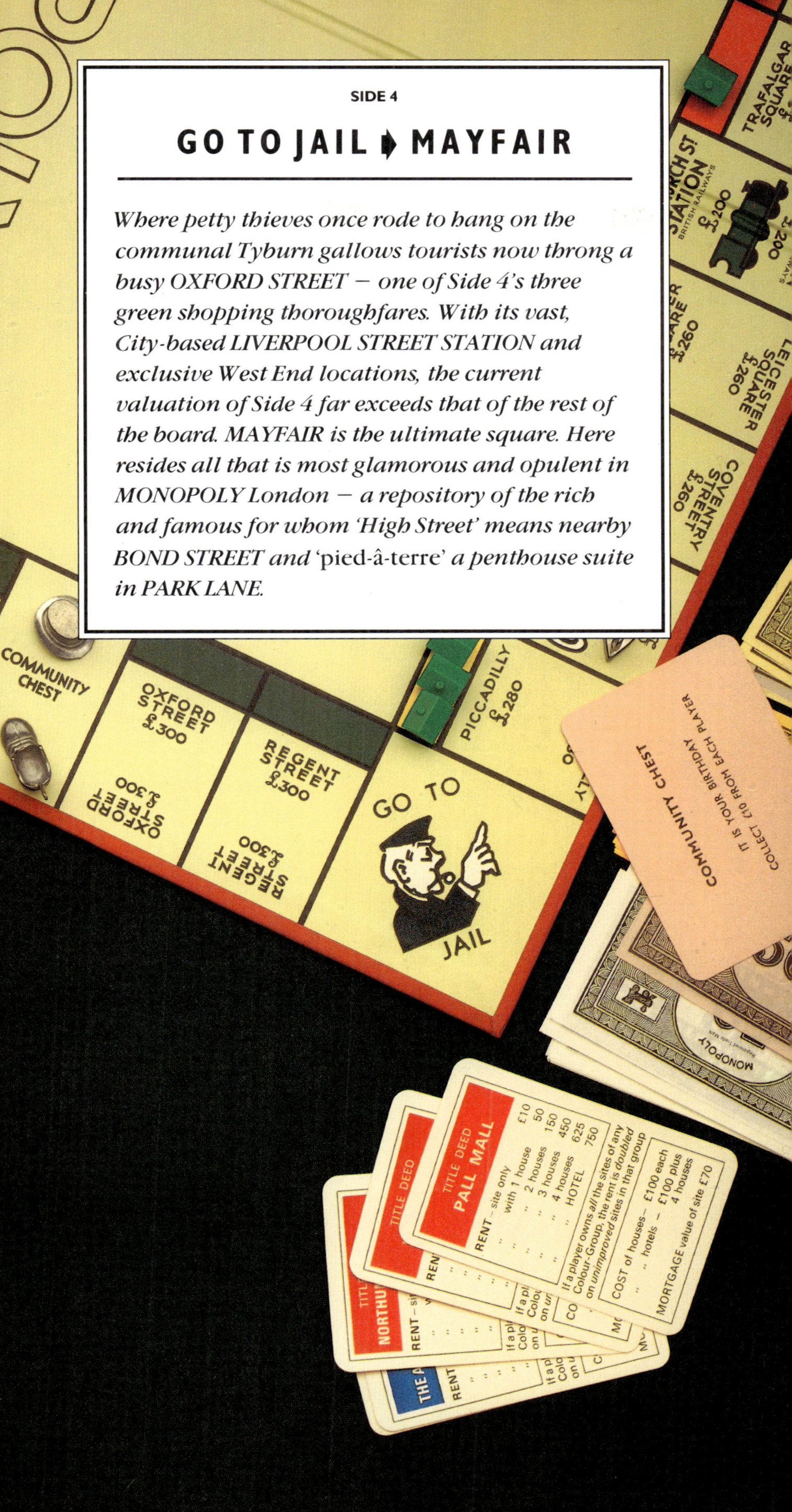

GO TO JAIL

Scotland Yard and the Metropolitan Police

'Ignorance of the law excuses no man; not that all men know the law, but because 'tis an excuse every man will plead, and no man can tell how to confute him.'

John Selden (1584-1654)

Many a murderous spine has been chilled by the whisper of Scotland Yard – dumb hero of countless films and thrillers usually based on the persevering detectives of today's world-famous Murder Squad. Yet Scotland Yard is much more than a back-drop for novelists. Founded in WHITEHALL, but now 1km further south, this is the nerve-centre for the capital's pioneering Metropolitan Police – the largest police force in the world covering an urban area of over 2,000km^2.

Until the early-19thC, law enforcement in London was haphazard. For centuries, night-watchmen and parish constables had made unco-ordinated attempts to maintain law and order; but no overall, official body of trained

and disciplined officers existed. By the late-18thC London was a rapidly expanding and increasingly lawless society. Then, in 1829, Home Secretary Sir Robert Peel successfully steered his Metropolitan Police Improvement Bill through Parliament, providing for the establishment of a regular police force for the capital. 1,000 men were recruited and grouped in six Divisions, controlled from #4 WHITEHALL Place, served by a courtyard whose

Home Secretary Robert Peel (1788-1850), architect of the Metropolitan Police in 1829, succeeded his father Sir Robert Peel (1750-1830) as 2nd Baronet in 1830. He was to hold office as Prime Minister from 1834 to 1835 and again from 1841 to 1846. Thrown from his horse on 29 June 1850, he was mortally wounded and died three days later.

name was to become synonymous with the most exacting standards of police detection work – Great Scotland Yard. On their first day of duty six of these new recruits were discharged for drunkenness. Yet, within a year their numbers had swelled to 3,000, working out of early police stations like VINE STREET. But Sir Robert Peel's 'Bobbies' or 'Peelers' were not popular. They were physically assaulted and savagely caricatured. The public, fearing loss of individual liberty, so detested and distrusted them that in 1831 a jury recorded a verdict of 'justifiable homicide' after one police constable, unarmed, had been stabbed to death during a riot.

Gradually, public attitudes to the police mellowed. Two assassination attempts against Queen Victoria provoked the institution in 1842 of a tiny, six-man Detective Department – forerunner of today's famous Criminal Investigation Department or CID. In 1883 the Special Irish Branch was formed to counter a series of explosions in London caused by Irish agitators. By 1901 the first telephone had been installed at Scotland Yard and the new science of fingerprinting introduced. In 1910 radio telegraphy made its début with the trans-Atlantic apprehension of the murderer, Dr Crippen. By 1920 motor vehicles had been introduced and radio communication between Scotland Yard and patrolling cars soon followed.

Today, the Metropolitan Police use a broad range of sophisticated scientific and technical equipment in the execution of their duty. Scotland Yard heads a complex organisation composed of specialist sections like the Mounted Branch, whose origins go back to the 18thC 'Robin Redbreasts'

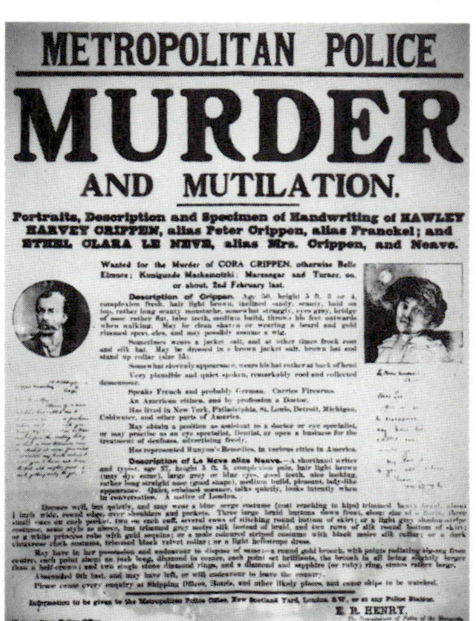

METROPOLITAN POLICE

MURDER

AND MUTILATION.

Portraits, Description and Specimen of Handwriting of HAWLEY HARVEY CRIPPEN, alias Peter Crippen, alias Franckel; and ETHEL CLARA LE NEVE, alias Mrs. Crippen, and Neave.

Wanted for the Murder of CORA CRIPPEN, otherwise Belle Elmore; Kunigunde Mackamotzki; Marsangar and Turner, on or about, 2nd February last.

Information to be given to the Metropolitan Police Office, New Scotland Yard, London S.W., or at any Police Station.

E. R. HENRY.

This Metropolitan Police 'Wanted' poster dated 16 July 1910 reveals that the 'American citizen' Hawley Harvey Crippen 'throws his feet outwards when walking' and was of 'somewhat slovenly appearance', His inamorata Ethel Clara Le Neve, 'a native of London', had a 'rather long straight nose (good shape)'.

The motor boats of Thames Division patrol a ninety kilometre stretch of river twenty-four hours a day. Waterloo Pier, the only floating police station in the world, is housed on a pontoon.

organised from BOW STREET; or Special Branch, descendant of the Special Irish Branch and shadowy subject of spy novels and television mystery series. Other sections include the Flying Squad, whose nickname 'the Sweeney' is short for Sweeney Todd – cockney rhyming slang for Flying Squad; Thames Division, the river police whose station at Waterloo Pier

Although parish constables sometimes patrolled with dogs as early as the 15thC, it was not until 1946 that the Metropolitan Police officially enlisted dogs to assist in police work.

just off the STRAND is the only floating police station in the world; the UK office of Interpol, the international police liaison organisation; and the Dog Section, responsible for more than 300 operational dogs working in London – from German Shepherds or Alsations to Airedales and Dobermanns. The Special Escort Group, formed in 1952, provide protocol and security escorts for visiting heads of state, while the Diplomatic Protection Group, formed in 1974, protect diplomatic premises in central London. Yet the Yard's most famous section is probably C1 Serious Crime Branch, itself split into specialized groups like the Drugs Squad, the Organised Crime Squad ('Gangbusters') and the internationally acclaimed Murder Squad – whose tenacious detectives may be flown anywhere in the world to ensure that the perpetrator of a murder committed under British jurisdiction – perhaps aboard a British ship on the high seas – will eventually GO TO JAIL.

Popular associations: Quality shops / airline offices / Christmas decorations

REGENT STREET

(WI, SWI / City of Westminster)

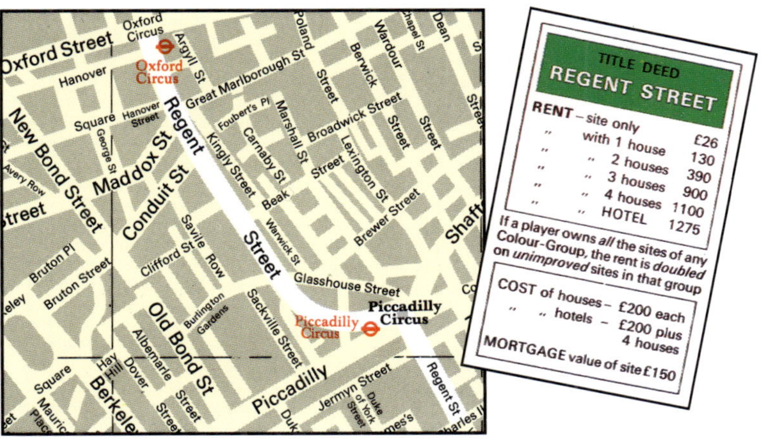

MONOPOLY valuation: £300
Current valuation: £525,000,000

Location description

All three streets in the MONOPOLY board's green property-group are pre-eminent among the shopping thoroughfares of London. REGENT STREET is the most princely of the three. From Langham Place and Oxford Circus it swathes south for 1km, approaching PICCADILLY Circus with the bold, classical sweep of the Quadrant for which it is perhaps most famed. From there it proceeds briefly as Lower REGENT STREET to Waterloo Place. Along this broad and gracious avenue – blue-blood MAYFAIR to the west, red-light Soho to the east – well-established stores and shops of great style and distinction mingle with airline and tourist offices of many nations.

Derivation of name

REGENT STREET takes its name from the Prince Regent for whom it was laid out in the early-19thC, forming but part of a grandiose scheme which included Regent's Park and Lower REGENT STREET.

Short history

REGENT STREET owes its being to a coincidental coupling of architectural genius and guileless royal vanity. In late-18thC West End London, already built-up and at times paralyzed by traffic congestion, proposals were voiced for a major new north-south artery. It did not escape the attention of the more astute Crown planners that such a new thoroughfare would increase the value of the 200ha Marylebone Park to the north, the leases for which were due to revert to the Crown in 1811. It fell to John Nash, by 1810 successful architect and influential adviser to the Prince Regent, to execute so audacious a scheme. Nash's plan would have perturbed many a modern

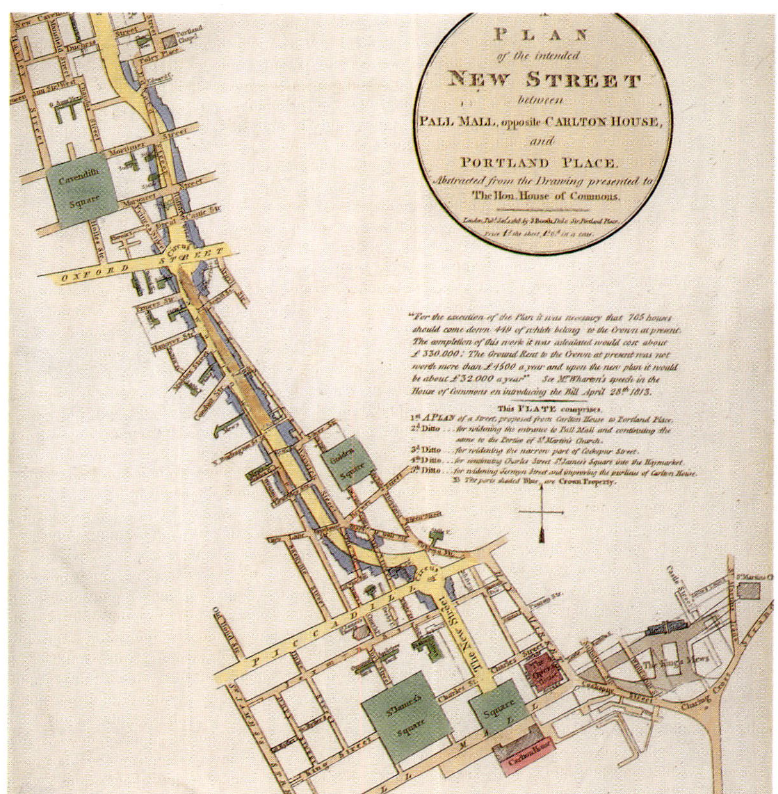

Contemporary plan for the REGENT STREET proposal. On its completion the ground rent to the crown, 'at present not worth more than £4500 a year', would rise to £32,000 a year. Notice that TRAFALGAR SQUARE has not yet been laid out.

sociologist, for it deliberately aggravated an existing class divide, throwing down a *cordon sanitaire* between the 'Streets and Squares occupied by the Nobility and Gentry [MAYFAIR], and the narrower Streets and meaner houses occupied by mechanics and the trading part of the community [Soho]'. From the Prince Regent's official residence in PALL MALL, this 'royal mile' was to drive northwards, largely following the route of the much older Swallow Street and Portland Place, linking royal Carlton House to the Marylebone estate. Regent's Park, as it became, was to be a garden city for the nobility with a summer villa for the Regent at its centre. Thus would the Crown be conveyed unsullied from palace to pavilion.

Work on REGENT STREET started in 1813, causing massive upheaval and disruption to business. Many existing streets were swept away or mutilated. Others were realigned or renamed. Great MARLBOROUGH STREET was extended westward. VINE STREET was all but annihilated; Swallow Street all but swallowed up. Nash struggled fiercely to maintain an elegant uniformity to all the façades. The straight, northern section of REGENT STREET was to be residential. The colonnades of the curving Quadrant, dedicated to stores of taste and distinction, sheltered shoppers and window-gazers from the vagaries of the weather; while from the balustrades above dashing male lodgers surveyed and conversed with 'those passing in the Carriages underneath'. Shopkeepers, artists and restaurateurs were soon eager to rent premises in the fashionable new street; but such architectural unity as Nash achieved was swept away within twenty years of his death – and the grand plan for Regent's Park was never completed.

Nash's original Quadrant, sweeping regally away from the present PICCADILLY Circus, was colonnaded with cast-iron columns.

Points of interest

Carlton House, which stood at the southern end of Lower REGENT STREET, was given by George III to his elder son, then Prince of Wales, later Prince Regent. Immediately the Prince set about its expansion and improvement. No expense was spared to create the 'most perfect palace in Europe'. Opulently furnished and exotically decorated, it was widely extolled. Yet when the Regent became monarch in 1820, the Carlton House that some had whispered in the same breath as Versailles was too modest for the King of England. Carlton House was swept away – to be replaced by Carlton House Terrace, splendid to this day; while the majestic residence that John Nash then fashioned for his regal patron was to become the world-famous Buckingham Palace.

Carlton House on the southern flank of PALL MALL. From here the Prince Regent had an uninterrupted view to the present PICCADILLY Circus, then called Regent Circus.

Shopping The shops of REGENT STREET fall somewhere between the mass appeal of OXFORD STREET and the select exclusivity of BOND STREET. These metaphors for quality and value have successfully preserved their traditional individuality: Aquascutum and Austin Reed for menswear; Garrard and Mappin & Webb for gold and jewellery; Liberty and Dickins & Jones for fine fabrics; Gered for bone china; Burberry's for trenchcoats; Hedges & Butler for wine; Lillywhites for sports-clothes. Other well-known names abound, like Boosey & Hawkes, publishers of music, Veeraswamy's, pioneer Indian restaurant, and the Café Royal, rendezvous of princes; while former venues like Verrey's Restaurant, patronised by Sherlock Holmes and Charles Dickens, once added to the colour and glamour of this elegant thoroughfare.

REGENT STREET's famous Café Royal dates from the 1860s when a Parisian wine merchant first opened a café-restaurant in Glasshouse Street. By the early-20thC the Café Royal had become a select redezvous patronised by the future kings Edward VIII and George VI for whom the waiters' standing instructions read: 'Always plain food. No fuss. Call head waiter at once and notify manager'.

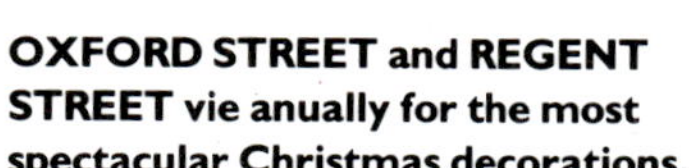

OXFORD STREET and REGENT STREET vie anually for the most spectacular Christmas decorations.

Hamleys of REGENT STREET (#188/196) is the largest toy shop in the world and something of a London institution. During the peak Christmas period up to 300 staff serve its 4,000m^2 of floor space spread over six floors. The original High Holborn shop, founded by William Hamley in 1760, was called Noah's Ark.

The **British Travel Centre** (#12 Lower REGENT STREET), established by the British Tourist Authority in 1986, is popular with visitors as a dependable source of information about London and the rest of Britain. Many other tourist agencies and international airline offices add to REGENT STREET's cosmopolitan atmosphere.

Famous people

The **Prince Regent** (1762-1830), for whom REGENT STREET and Regent's Park were laid out, acceded to the throne as George IV in 1820. For the preceding decade he had ruled as Regent with his usual great aplomb, his father's mind having become cruelly unhinged by 1811. As Prince, then as Regent and finally as King he was flamboyant, cultured and exorbitantly extravagant – detested by a hard-pressed nation locked for years in a bitter war against Napoleon. He had 'all the vices of the time, and practically every vice he carried to excess'. Yet the REGENT STREET scheme in its original form, Carlton House and the Brighton Pavilion all testify that what he lacked in virtue he atoned for in style.

This savage 1792 cartoon of the future George IV is captioned: 'A VOLUPTUARY under the horrors of Digestion'.

John Nash (1752-1835), pocket-architect to the Prince Regent and chief protagonist of the REGENT STREET scheme, was a self-made 'architectural impresario' who dreamed on a grand scale. He left his masterly mark in one way or another on much of London, including Buckingham Palace, Marble Arch and TRAFALGAR SQUARE. This short, unhandsome genius came to public attention and won royal favour through his imaginative designs for country houses and helpful marriage in 1798 to Mary Anne Bradley, one of the Regent's comely young mistresses. REGENT STREET was accomplished in the twilight of Nash's life, financed largely from his own considerable resources – amassed through hard work and natural brilliance following an early bankruptcy.

Sidney Reilly (1874-1925), Russian-born British master-spy who disappeared mysteriously in Russia after 1925, lunched regularly in the summer months of 1919 with MI5 agents at REGENT STREET's Café Royal. In his nearby bachelor chambers at Albany, PICCADILLY, this fast-living bigamist entertained a galaxy of diplomatic, military and political friends.

Popular associations: Department stores / street-traders / Christmas lights

OXFORD STREET

(W1/City of Westminster)

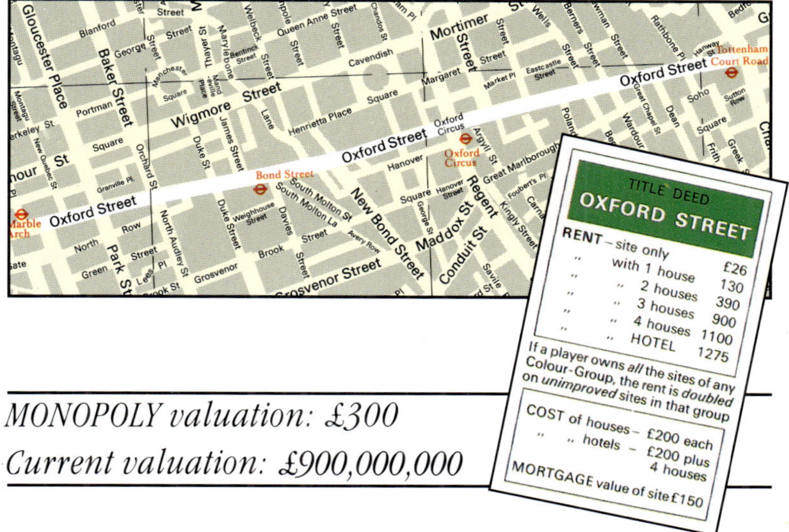

MONOPOLY valuation: £300
Current valuation: £900,000,000

Location description

One of the oldest routes on the MONOPOLY board, OXFORD STREET today runs 2km east-west between Tottenham Court Road and Marble Arch, pausing briefly at Oxford Circus to intersect REGENT STREET. For centuries a rural, west-bound highway out of London, OXFORD STREET is now a thriving shopping centre at the very heart of the metropolis. This broad, straight thoroughfare of renowned department stores, established chain outlets and trendy boutiques is probably London's busiest and most celebrated shopping scene – the High Street of the capital. The crowds that routinely throng its vast stores are swelled in summer by countless tourists attracted by its more or less legal street-traders whose stalls abound with colourful fruits and sparkling souvenirs.

Derivation of name

OXFORD STREET seems to have derived its name in two ways. Before the 18thC it had been known variously as 'The Waye to Uxbridge', the 'King's Highway' and 'Tyburn Way'. Yet it had also been called the 'Road to Oxford' by virtue of one of its destinations. Then the term 'OXFORD STREET' itself came into use in the 18thC when it was named after Robert Harley, 1st Earl of Oxford, who coincidentally owned much of the adjacent land.

Short history

Present OXFORD STREET follows part of the route of an ancient Roman road from Suffolk to Hampshire. Together with modern PICCADILLY it was for centuries one of the two principal routes westward out of London – a deep, rutted, country lane, worked in places by cut-throats and highwaymen. Not until the early-1700s did it begin to be built up in the east; yet by the end of the century its entire length had been transformed from rural lane to city artery, a continuous line of mostly residential properties. Foreign visitors were deeply impressed by the oil-lamps that glowed by law outside each house – more lamps than in the whole of Paris. Later came shops to serve the many households with furniture, clothing, drapery. And later still, at the turn of the 20thC, came the giant department stores that are a characteristic feature of the street today.

Up to twenty-one convicts could be hanged simultanously on Tyburn's triangular gallows. In Hogarth's grim 18thC commentary, *The Idle 'Prentice Executed at Tyburn*, the foremost of the countless spectators holds in her hands 'The last dying Speech & Confession of – The Idle'.

Points of interest

Tyburn gallows The 'Tyburn Tree', set in green fields near the present Marble Arch and used as early as the 12thC, became London's principal location for public hangings until 1783. By the late-1500s a permanent, triangular structure had been erected, from which up to twenty-one convicts could be suspended simultaneously. Public hangings excited considerable public interest, attracting spectators by the thousand – sometimes by the hundred thousand. The practice was to bring prisoners to the gallows in a cart, usually along modern OXFORD STREET, stopping for beer at taverns *en route*. By the time the rope caressed a prisoner's neck, alcohol had often seduced his mind. The hangman, sometimes himself drunk, would whip the horse and cart away and, if the dangling man was fortunate, friends would hasten the end by pulling at his legs and beating his chest. Hangings – sometimes enlivened by drawing and quartering – were highly profitable for some. As well as having the right to the prisoner's clothes, the hangman would sell the genuine execution rope by the inch; sharpsters in Tyburn Road would sell the 'same' rope at half the price; while an 18thC Mrs Proctor made a fortune by erecting a stadium and charging for seats.

Selfridges dominates the western end of OXFORD STREET, its reiterative Ionic columns striving to honour Gordon Selfridge's conviction that great business houses should 'unite beauty' with their effort.

Department stores OXFORD STREET is unquestionably the home of the reasonably-priced London department store. West of Oxford Circus the street abounds with household names like British Home Stores, C & A, Debenhams, D H Evans, John Lewis and Littlewoods. But two names above all are famous to tourists: the monumental Selfridges, founded in 1909 by the American, Harry Gordon Selfridge – London's equivalent to New York's Macy's; and the legendary Marks & Spencer, whose *St Michael* brassières are allegedly worn by two out of every three women in Britain.

The Queen of Time accompanies Selfridge's famous clock – surmounted over the store's main entrance.

The **Pantheon**, opened in 1772 on the site of the present Marks and Spencer, was widely regarded as 'the most elegant structure in Europe, if not on the globe'. In this enchanted temple of recreation – with its exquisite rotunda, its card rooms, tea rooms and delicately stuccoed ceilings – masked balls, fêtes, exhibitions and concerts were regularly held. But in the winter of 1792 the beautiful building that took nearly three years to erect was destroyed by fire in a single night. In the bitter January frost the water-jets from the fire engines froze in the air. It was, perhaps, a gratifying sight for the owners of the King's Theatre, Haymarket, whispered by the malicious to have started the fire: but a painful one for those who loved the Pantheon. Although rebuilt in 1792, the style, grace and glamour of those early years could never be recaptured, and it was eventually dismantled in 1937.

Famous people

Jack Sheppard (1702-24) By the age of twenty-two, when he was hanged at Tyburn for robbery, Jack Sheppard had already achieved immortality. Caught and imprisoned in April 1724, he escaped four times within the next few months. Finally, he was caught while drunk and watched day and night until his execution in November, when 200,000 Londoners came to watch this popular anti-hero make his final exit.

Thomas de Quincey (1785-1859), English writer, adventurer and opium addict, bought his first dose of opium at an OXFORD STREET pharmacy next to the Pantheon. His *Confessions of an Opium-Eater* contains bitter references to 'stony-hearted' OXFORD STREET.

Hawley Harvey Crippen (1862-1910), the London-based American poisoner, pawned his murdered wife's jewels in Adam & Eve Court just off OXFORD STREET. Dr Crippen had the misfortune to be the first murderer apprehended through the use of radio telegraphy. Fleeing with his secretary/mistress on board a transatlantic liner, Crippen aroused the suspicions of the ship's captain who used his new-fangled wireless to contact Scotland Yard. As the fugitives disembarked at Quebec they were arrested by an English detective who had taken a faster ship. Crippen was later hanged at Pentonville Prison.

Stanley Green (b1915), endearingly eccentric vegetarian whose sandwich-boards declare 'less lust from less protein', is a famous, roving landmark in the OXFORD STREET panorama. Since 1968, when he was fifty-three, Stanley Green has been patrolling the pavements of OXFORD STREET 'between one Marks & Spencer and the other'. Nightly he hand prints and staples the booklets that he sells daily for a few pence each. His simple message – protein makes passion: passion makes torment – has been seen by millions from across the globe.

COMMUNITY CHEST

FROM SALE OF STOCK YOU GET £50

Did you know . . . that the London Stock Exchange lists almost twice as many companies as any other stock exchange in the world, with a total market capitalisation of over £1,500,000,000,000.

GET OUT OF JAIL FREE

Did you know . . . that in 1101 Rannulf Flambard, Bishop of Durham, became both the first prisoner and the first escapee of the Tower of London. From a cask of smuggled wine, with which he intoxicated his guards, Flambard took a concealed rope – making his departure through a window.

INCOME TAX REFUND COLLECT £20

Did you know . . . that INCOME TAX was first introduced in Great Britain in 1799 at a standard rate of 2s (10p) in the £?

PAY YOUR INSURANCE PREMIUM

Did you know . . . that the largest life assurance group in the UK is the City of London's life assurance pioneer, the Prudential Corporation, with a total amount assured of nearly £100,000,000,000.

IT IS YOUR BIRTHDAY COLLECT £10 FROM EACH PLAYER

Did you know that . . . the Trooping the Colour – performed annually on Horse Guards Parade in WHITEHALL to mark the sovereign's official birthday – has been held regularly since 1805, and sporadically since 1755.

Popular associations: Luxury shops / fine art auctioneers / galleries

BOND STREET

(W1/City of Westminster)

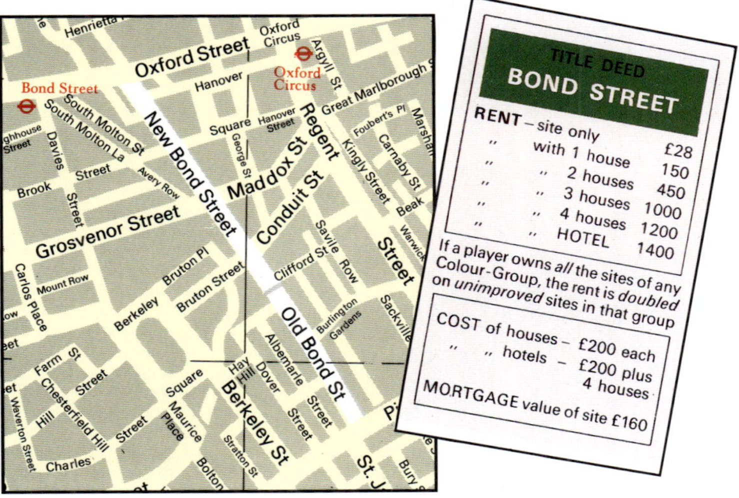

MONOPOLY valuation: £320
Current valuation: £306,000,000

Location description

The most refined of the three green shopping streets on the MONOPOLY board, quaint, straight and narrow BOND STREET dissects MAYFAIR. Setting off northwards from PICCADILLY as 'Old' BOND STREET, it arrives after 1km at OXFORD STREET in the guise of 'New' BOND STREET. Its quiet, jumbled and unremarkable buildings exude an indefinable air of glamour and distinction. In this most understated of English thoroughfares, the High Street of MAYFAIR, expensive French couture mingles with exquisite jewellery, sophisticated perfumes with international art, elegant leather goods with priceless silver.

Derivation of name

Old BOND STREET was originally plain BOND STREET, taking its name from the 17thC financier, Sir Thomas Bond, a member of the consortium which invested heavily in its development. When the street was extended, the two parts were then named Old and New.

Short history

The 200m Old BOND STREET was laid out in about 1686 by Sir Thomas Bond and a goldsmith named John Hinde. But it was not until the 1720s that the Earl of Oxford completed New BOND STREET as far as OXFORD STREET. The rapid expansion of MAYFAIR, and the drift of the principal shopping areas away from the City to the West End, enhanced the reputation that BOND STREET soon acquired as a luxury shopping street. Open market-stalls were giving way to enclosed stores, the proprietor living over the shop, his assistant sleeping under the counter. Other rooms in this stylish new street were rented to lodgers, often with illustrious names like the satirist Jonathan Swift or the statesman William Pitt the Elder.

Cartier – among the world's most select jewellers at #175-176 New BOND STREET – were first established in Burlington Street in 1902.

Points of interest

Shopping in BOND STREET is not for the fainthearted. This is a street in which prices are seldom marked and never asked. Patronised by British and foreign monarchs, past and present, its 24-carat names justly evoke a world of grace and opulence: Chanel for perfume; Cartier and Asprey for jewellery: Karl Lagerfeld for feminine fashion, Hermes for gentlemen's attire and St Laurent for both; Rayne and Gucci for footwear; Patek Philippe for the politeness of kings. In the art galleries of BOND STREET and the surrounding area, old masters and the cream of contemporary paintings are displayed and sold. Famous names like Thomas Agnew & Son – founded in 1817 – and Wildenstein – established in Paris in 1875 – add lustre to the district's unparalleled reputation in the world of international art.

Sotheby's (#34/35 New) Together with Christie's in nearby King Street, the name of Sotheby's ranks among the world's most esteemed and celebrated of fine art auctioneers. First established in 1744 for the sale of books, its present small and unremarkable façade masks a larger, fantasy world of priceless paintings and *objets d'art* where the sale of individual lots for eight-figure values is increasingly commonplace. The smaller but equally respected fine art auctioneers – Phillips, founded in 1796 – are at Blenstock House, New BOND STREET.

In the elegant Royal Arcade, opened in 1879 between old BOND STREET and Albemarle Street, Queen Victoria used to buy her handkerchiefs and vests.

Many of the world's most exclusive names have become established in BOND STREET. Celine of Paris at #28 New BOND STREET and Loewe at #25 Old BOND STREET are both esteemed for their high class leather and suede merchandise. The Spanish company Loewe was founded in Madrid in 1846.

Famous people

Laurence Sterne (1713-68), popular novelist and author of the *Life and Opinions of Tristram Shandy,* died in Old BOND STREET at the 'silk-bag shop'. Putting his hand up as if to fend off a blow, he died of pleurisy with the words 'Now it is come'. His belongings were plundered by his own servants and his body snatched from its tomb by grave-robbers.

Edward Gibbon (1737-94), 'most celebrated of the world's historians', lodged in BOND STREET as a young man of twenty-one. In later life Gibbon composed his magnum opus, the classic *Decline and Fall of the Roman Empire* which was, over a century later, to influence the literary style and political thinking of the young Winston Churchill.

Charles James Fox (1749-1806), fast-living English statesman, heavy drinker and reckless gambler, one day gambled with the future Prince Regent as to the number of cats they might count on either side of BOND STREET. Not always lucky in gambling, having lost a fortune at cards and dice, on this occasion he outfoxed the prince handsomely. Having opted for the sunny side of BOND STREET, the debonair Fox counted thirteen, the prince none.

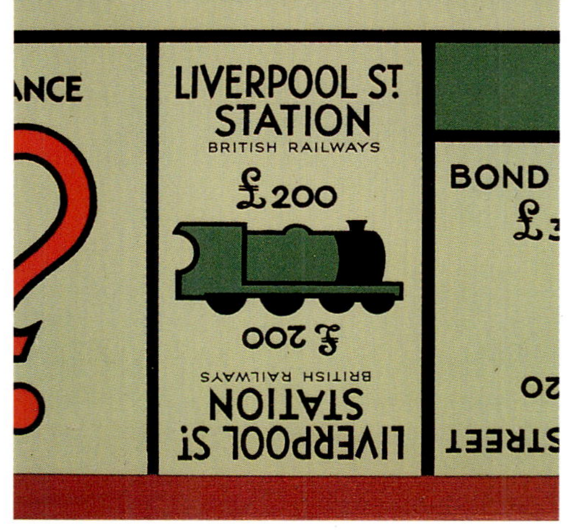

LIVERPOOL S^T STATION

(Liverpool Street, EC2/City of London)

Temple of the Great Eastern Railway and vast passenger terminus for British Rail's Eastern Region, LIVERPOOL STREET STATION is the busiest terminus in London.

MONOPOLY valuation: £200
Current valuation: £1,920,000,000

Opening date

1874

Principal destinations

Include Cambridge, Colchester, Harwich, Ipswich, Lowestoft, Norwich, Southend, Stansted Airport

Traffic statistics

Passenger trains daily: 1,130
Passengers daily: 160,000

Station background

In 1840 the Eastern Counties Railway opened Shoreditch Station, a dismal, inconvenient terminus 0.75km to the north of the present LIVERPOOL STREET STATION. For incoming passengers – prosperous merchants and businessmen of the City – it was a grim portal to London, sited outside the City precincts in an area infested by 'pickpockets, housebreakers and prostitutes'. Even its change of name in 1846 to the healthier sounding Bishopsgate Station did not improve its prospects.

When the Eastern Counties Railway became part of the Great Eastern Railway in 1862, the directors sought to extend the Shoreditch lines and build a new, more imposing terminus within the City. Eventually approval was given for the construction of a cryptic, low-level station at Liverpool Street – hardly the bold, bespired, high-level terminus that the directors had envisaged advancing to the very bounds of London Wall. In 1874 this new, £2,000,000, Victorian-Gothic extravaganza opened for business.

Development of traffic was staggering. When, in 1894, the station's original nine platforms were extended to eighteen, LIVERPOOL STREET STATION – already the busiest station in London – became also the largest. The extension was fronted by the new Great Eastern Hotel, serviced originally by a subterranean line whose troglodytic, nocturnal trains delivered coal and bath-time sea water, and carried away refuse and ashes.

LIVERPOOL STREET STATION
decorated for the coronation.

Within the first decade of the new century LIVERPOOL STREET STATION was handling 1,000 train movements daily; and throughout the century its traffic continued to grow, at one time reaching more than 200,000 passengers daily. In the mid-1980s work started on a massive, 168 hours-a-week project destined to create the largest building site in Europe – the ultimate goal, a 21stC rail centre for LIVERPOOL STREET STATION and a major office/leisure complex at adjacent but obsolete Broad Street Station.

During the peak morning period 59,000 pasengers disembark daily at LIVERPOOL STREET STATION.

Station timetable

1840: Shoreditch Station established by Eastern Counties Railway.
1862: Eastern Counties Railway merges with Great Eastern Railway.
1874 (2 February): 0.75km extension from Shoreditch completed. LIVERPOOL STREET STATION opens for suburban traffic.
1875 (1 November): LIVERPOOL STREET STATION opens for all business.
1884: Great Eastern Hotel erected.
1894: LIVERPOOL STREET STATION enlarged for additional traffic. Platforms increased to eighteen.
1902: annual total of journeys through LIVERPOOL STREET STATION reaches 65,000,000.
1914-18 (First World War): substantial military traffic. Serious damage and many fatalities.
1917: connection to Underground.
1920: Intensive Service commuter trains – nicknamed the 'Jazz Service' – introduced.
1923: Great Eastern Railway becomes part of London and North Eastern Railway – carrying the densest steam-operated suburban service in the world.
1927: Post Office railway connection.
1939-45 (Second World War): much loss of life and severe damage inflicted by enemy bombing.
1949: first electrification lines go live.
1962: last steam train departs LIVERPOOL STREET STATION.
1986: contractors start work on LIVERPOOL STREET STATION redevelopment.
1987: electrification to Cambridge and Norwich.
1991: LIVERPOOL STREET STATION redevelopment completed.

CHANCE

ADVANCE TO MAYFAIR

In which MAYFAIR street did Bertie Wooster live with his famous man-servant Jeeves?

a) Brook Street
b) Shepherd Street
c) Half Moon Street

BANK PAYS YOU DIVIDEND OF £50

Which of the following areas is celebrated as a centre of banking and high finance?

a) City of Westminster
b) London Borough of Camden
c) City of London

ADVANCE TO "GO"

In which year did the Romans under Aulus Plautius found Londinium, the modern City of London?

a) 55BC
b) AD43
c) AD410

GET OUT OF JAIL FREE

At which prison could inmates pay for better accommodation and special privileges?

a) Pentonville Prison
b) Fleet Prison
c) BOW STREET Prison

TAKE A TRIP TO MARYLEBONE STATION AND IF YOU PASS "GO" COLLECT £200

You might travel from MARYLEBONE STATION if you wished to visit which of the following destinations?

a) Aberdeen
b) High Wycombe
c) Cambridge

answers: ccbbb

PARK LANE

(W1/City of Westminster)

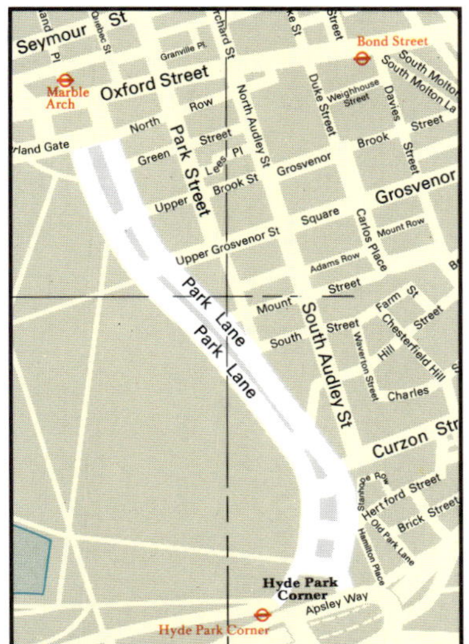

MONOPOLY valuation: £350
Current valuation: £720,000,000

Location description

'His taste in residence is plain:
No palaces his heart rejoice:
A cottage in a lane (PARK LANE for choice) – '

Alfred Denis Godley (1856-1925) *Lyra Frivola* 'After Horace'

The broadest of all the MONOPOLY streets, and one of the most famous in the world, PARK LANE is today a 1.2km dual-carriageway boulevard linking the western extremities of OXFORD STREET and PICCADILLY. The park that it skirts and the graceful plane trees that it enjoys lend an open, almost rural aspect to London's only eight-lane highway, as its high-volume traffic speeds relentlessly past opulent car showrooms and lofty, palatial hotels.

Derivation of name

PARK LANE takes its name directly from the 140-hectare Hyde Park, the eastern border of which it forms.

Short history

Before the development of MAYFAIR, PARK LANE was a leafy country bridle-path on the eastern boundary of Hyde Park. Early maps show it as Tyburn Lane, taking its name from the Tyburn stream. Then, in the mid-1700s, a few noble mansions were scattered on its east side. Facing away from Tyburn Lane, they were entered from the more salubrious Park Street which ran, then as now, parallel and a little to the east. Gradually grand houses were built facing the park, and the original name, with its gruesome echo of the Tyburn gallows, was quietly forgotten. Soon, the lane became a highly sought-after address, attracting the wealthy and aristocratic. In the mid-1960s PARK LANE was transformed by the addition of a second carriageway to the west at the expense of a generous ribbon of parkland. Today most of the great houses have gone, their memory preserved by the early-20thC five-star hotels that supplanted them; while to the south, mid/late-20thC hotels tower over Hyde Park, resculpturing the London skyline and compromising the privacy of nearby Buckingham Palace gardens.

Opening of the Great Exhibition of 1851 seen from beyond the Serpentine.

Points of interest

The royal **Hyde Park** and Kensington Gardens, clearly discernible in satellite photographs from an altitude of over 700km, extend for well over 2km to the west of PARK LANE. In 1536 the ubiquitous Henry VIII confiscated the estates of Westminster Abbey, including the property of Hyde to the west of Tudor London. Roamed as it was by wild boar and deer, Henry and subsequent monarchs used the new Crown property as a convenient hunting park. It became variously a fashionable playground, a haunt of highwaymen and a stage for duels. The deceptively named **Serpentine** was created in the 1730s, a modestly kinked, artificial lake covering 16ha. In 1851 the fairy-tale Crystal Palace was erected, a spectacular iron and glass edifice housing the Great Exhibition of Industry of All Nations. On the night of 30 November 1936, after its re-erection in South London, fire mysteriously

Above: Orators usually find willing if transient listeners at Speakers' Corner.
Left: Marble Arch was modelled in 1827 on the Arch of Constantine in Rome at a cost of £10,000.

razed the glistening palace – a potential beacon, so it was whispered, for future night-time bombers seeking landmarks in a blacked-out city. At **Speakers' Corner**, established in the north-east angle of Hyde Park following riots of the mid-19thC, orators exercise their right to declaim on a wide variety of topics, sometimes political, sometimes religious, often eccentric.

Marble Arch, at the northern extremity of PARK LANE, was built in 1828 by John Nash to adorn the entrance to Buckingham Palace. It was brought to its present site in 1851 and surrendered to the ceaseless encircling traffic in 1908. **Hyde Park Corner**, at the opposing end of PARK LANE, falls equal prey to unending traffic. When Knightsbridge and Kensington were outlying enclaves this was ever London's western entrance, barred by toll-gate. Here the 18thC **Apsley House** – once loftily known as 'Number 1 London' and palatial home of Britain's illustrious Iron Duke – exhibits an impressive collection of Wellingtoniana.

Hotels The plush, titanic hotels that seem so integral a feature of PARK LANE today are in reality fledglings in an historic landscape. Yet the grandest of them echo authentically the grace and luxury of the households they succeeded. From their portals emerge dynastic rulers and foreign potentates, glittering film stars and self-made tycoons, distinguished ambassadors and grand politicians. The Grosvenor House, opened in 1928, was London's first hotel to be equipped with a swimming pool. It is celebrated for its vast banqueting room – converted from a 1930s skating

The Dorchester's sound reinforced concrete construction lent itself to the strength and security necessary for General Eisenhower's London headquarters during the Second World War.

rink – which doubled as a wartime officers' mess for American servicemen billeted here. The Dorchester, opened in 1931, served as London headquarters for General Eisenhower. With its opulent roof-garden suites and exalted *haute cuisine* Terrace restaurant, the Dorchester – now owned by the Sultan of Brunei – is destined to become the 'most luxurious hotel in the world'. At 30-storeys the Hilton is one of London's tallest buildings. Built in 1963, its roofline bars command spectacular views over the parkland where Henry VIII once hunted deer. Nearby, the Londonderry was built in the 1960s on the site of 18thC Londonderry House. The Inn on the Park – an opulent modern hotel furnished with impressive antiques – was built in 1970; while the American-style Intercontinental opened in 1975.

A liveried doorman at the Dorchester, a limousine at the Hilton – symbols of wealth and influence common to PARK LANE.

Famous people

Benjamin Disraeli (1804-81), formidable British statesman and prolific novelist, lived at #93 from 1839 until his wife's death in 1872. His first novel, *Vivian Grey,* was published in 1826 and made him famous overnight. From 1830-40 he published a torrent of fiction and lived as a fashionable young man about town. Two years before moving to PARK LANE, Disraeli had entered Parliament. His maiden speech was drowned in derisive laughter, prompting his famous and prophetic closing words: 'Though I sit down now, the time will come when you will hear me.'

Howard Hughes (1905-76), eccentric American zillionaire obsessed with privacy and personal hygiene, lived on PARK LANE in impoverished isolation after taking over two complete floors of the star-spangled Inn on the Park hotel. Incarcerated in walled-off hotel suites for the last twenty years of his life, the reclusive Hughes master-minded a vast, far-flung business empire, shambling around a Kleenex-carpeted bedroom and shunning contact with all but his bodyguard.

Howard Hughes as Hollywood producer, seen with the short-lived Jean Harlow whom he created with his 1930 film *Hell's Angels.*

Earl Mountbatten of Burma (1900-79), British statesman, admiral and last viceroy of India, lived in PARK LANE for some years. The Mountbattens owned one of London's first penthouses on the seventh floor of Brook House at the corner of Upper Brook Street. The nautical earl's bedroom was modelled on a captain's cabin, complete with brass ship's clock and screw-down furniture. At the turn of his ninth decade this wartime Chief of Combined Operations, Supreme Allied Commander in South-East Asia, Viceroy of India, First Sea Lord and personal aide-de-camp to the Queen was slain by Irish terrorists while sailing at his country home in County Sligo.

SUPER TAX PAY £100

SUPER TAX is appropriately sandwiched between the two most exclusive spaces on the MONOPOLY board. Yet to the relief of many of the wealthy residents of PARK LANE and MAYFAIR this punitive levy – with its grim promise of near 100% taxation – was a relatively short-lived affair abandoned in the early 1970s.

Although the STRAND-based Board of Inland Revenue at Somerset House used to be responsible for the administration and collection of SUPER TAX, it was Her Majesty's Treasury – at the southern end of WHITEHALL – who had overall control. The British Prime Minister is also First Lord of the Treasury, but the Chancellor of the Exchequer – whose official residence is at #11 Downing Street – has day to day responsibility for the Treasury.

It was a Liberal Chancellor of the Exchequer, David Lloyd George, who introduced SUPER TAX in his highly contentious budget of 1909. His intention was two-fold: firstly to finance old age pensions as part of a social reform programme; and secondly, to finance the expansion of Britain's navy to counter Germany's growing naval adventurism.

SUPER TAX was imposed on top of the highest rate of INCOME TAX – initially at 6d in the £ (2.5%) on incomes over £5,000 per annum. In 1928 it was renamed Surtax and by 1948 had reached its peak – a punishing 10s 6d in the £ (52.5%) – to finance the introduction of Britain's 'welfare state'. Since the top rate of INCOME TAX at that time was 9s in the £ (45%), patrons of Surtax paid the legendary combined rate of 19s 6d in the £ (97.5%).

David Lloyd George (1863-1945) photographed c1915. Lloyd George's renowned 'people's budget' of 1909 set out to redistribute wealth in favour of the working and at the expense of the landowning classes. His SUPER TAX budget was rejected by the House of Lords, creating a constitutional crisis that resulted in the Parliament Act of 1911.

MAYFAIR

(W1/City of Westminster)

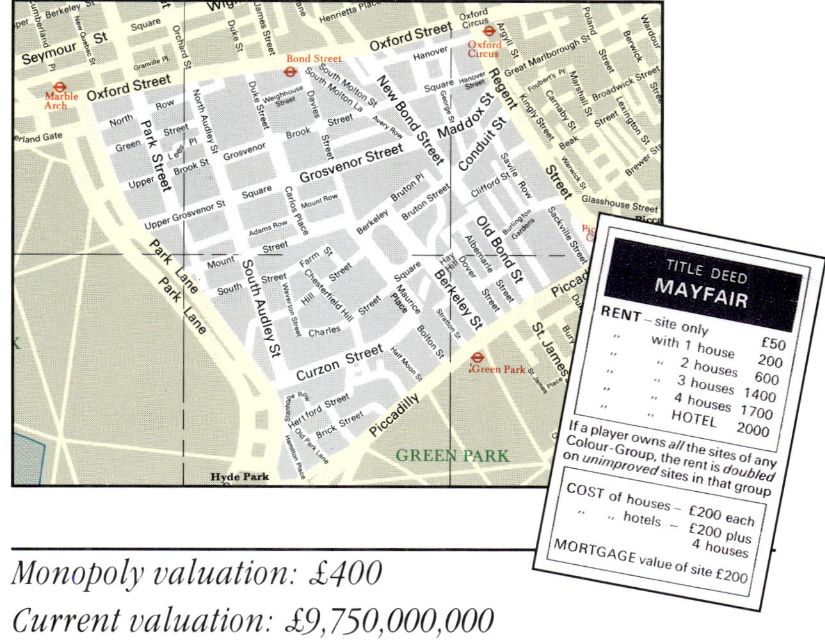

Monopoly valuation: £400
Current valuation: £9,750,000,000

Location description

Historically, MAYFAIR has been considered to lie within an area bounded by OXFORD STREET to the north, PICCADILLY to the south, REGENT STREET to the east and PARK LANE to the west; today, however, there is a tendency to regard BOND STREET as its eastern boundary. The area is synonymous with opulence and glamour, exuding an air of quiet exclusivity. Within it are tree-filled squares and elegant terraces; large, Georgian houses and miniature mews; and limousine-lined streets with expensive shops, discreet casinos, exquisite galleries, sumptuous restaurants, hurrying call-girls and luxurious hotels: all serving the rich and the nouveaux-riches, the aristocratic and the diplomatic, the famous and the infamous. MAYFAIR justly deserves its reputation as the most expensive space on the MONOPOLY board.

Derivation of name

Although not officially recognised as a district within London, the name MAYFAIR survives an earlier fifteen-day fair, an annual scene of debauchery held in this area each May and suppressed at the end of the 18thC.

Short history

The disreputable May Fair started nearly a mile away in 1290 at the gates of what eventually became St James's Palace, but which had been since Norman times a hospital for female lepers. The proceeds of the fair helped towards

'May Fair in 1716'. Nearly one hundred years later the noise, stench and nefarious goings-on at this annual saturnalia were to lead to its suppression.

the upkeep of the colony, until King Henry VIII pensioned off the last three inmates and turned the leper hospital into a royal residence. In the late-17thC the old fair was gradually edged out to lush, green meadows on the western outskirts of London, overlooked from afar by a newly built Old BOND STREET. Entertainments included singing and dancing, performances from strolling players, displays of wild animals and liberal carousing and revelry. One early-18thC visitor to the teeming fair could not find 'one man that looked above the degree of Gentleman's Valet, nor one whore that could have the Impudence to ask above sixpence for an hour of her cursed company.'

In 1738 architect Edward Sheppard obtained a grant to build a cattle-market in the centre of the fair-ground and for about thirty years the spring-time carnival continued with the market as its rallying centre. But the 6th Earl of Coventry, whose garden wall overlooked the noisy, congested scenes of revelry, was able, through his position, to deal a death blow to the annual May Fair in the reign of George III.

The street plan that evolved on and around the fields of the 18thC May Fair is still recognisable, although there was extensive 19thC rebuilding by Thomas Cubitt. MAYFAIR, invaded by the aristocracy, became synonymous with glamour and blue-blooded high life; and its grand mansions held their own until the eruption of the First World War and the passing of an age of grace. Today, although rich in examples of fine 18thC houses, inflationary property prices have eroded MAYFAIR's residential areas until little but company flats and luxury apartments rented to itinerant foreigners remain for private occupation.

Points of interest

MAYFAIR Chapel In this once notorious chapel near Hertford Street a disreputable clergyman – Dr Alexander Keith – would, without banns or licence, marry anyone for a guinea at any hour of the day or night. According to the parish records 6,000 illegal marriages took place here. The most sensational such union was that of James Duke of Hamilton to the arrestingly beautiful Miss Elizabeth Gunning on St Valentine's Day 1752. After meeting her at a Chesterfield House reception, the young duke married her with the ring of a bed-curtain at half-past midnight. Unlawful marriages in MAYFAIR and other parts of London became such a scandal that Parliament ended them with the Marriage Act of 1754 (prompting, instead, the popularity of Gretna Green in Scotland).

Hanover Square (built 1715-1750) is the oldest of MAYFAIR's squares. Its huge bronze statue of William Pitt was nearly pulled down by radicals as soon as it was erected in 1831. **St George Hanover Square**, built in 1724, has always been associated with the flashiest of weddings. Down its aisle have trod Emma and Sir William Hamilton, Shelley when he married Harriet Westbrook, Disraeli, George Elliot, Theodore Roosevelt and the Asquiths (at whose wedding four prime ministers signed the register). The roll-call continues today, with pop-stars and politicians, dukes and diplomats sharing its broad and colonnaded steps.

MAYFAIR

Shepherd Market, Shepherd Street, Shepherds Tavern: these names at MAYFAIR's village centre recall the 18thC architect and builder who was so prolific in this area – Edward Sheppard aka Shepherd.

Grosvenor Square, the largest of MAYFAIR's open spaces, was laid out c1725 by Sir Richard Grosvenor on the site of Oliver's Mount, an earthen defence erected by Cromwell's forces in 1643 during the Civil War as Charles I marched on the capital. Today, under its massive, brooding eagle, the United States Embassy dominates the entire western end of this 'Little America'. Uniform terraces surround the rest of the square, housing the diplomatic and administrative offices of the United States. In the open 6-acre garden stands a memorial to President Franklin D Roosevelt; and in #20 General Eisenhower set up wartime headquarters.

Berkeley Square, in whose leafy glades a nightingale sang, is well stocked with magnificent plane trees, some of them nearly 200 years old. Built c1739 on part of the former Berkeley House gardens, this was once one of the most blue-blooded of London Squares. Although 20thC rebuilding has destroyed much of its earlier elegance, the square still retains some attractive 18thC houses in its SW corner. #44 – now the Clermont Club, a fashionable casino – has been described by Nikolaus Pevsner as 'the finest terrace house of London', although the façade only hints at the interior grandeur. As with so many 18thC houses the interior and exterior are impeccably proportioned.

After the Restoration, Lord Berkeley of Stratton – the Royalist commander in the Civil War – procured much land north of PICCADILLY, including the present Berkeley Square seen here in autumn. Nearby names like Berkeley Street and Stratton Street help to perpetuate the commander's memory.

Above: Brown's Hotel in Dover Street, with its charm and privacy, still enjoys the Victorian Britishness inculcated by its 19thC founder. Left: Crockford's in Curzon Street is a private club and casino the origins of which may be traced to 1828 when William Crockford established an exclusive gambling house in St James's Street patronised by the 'chief aristocracy of England'.

Hotels The three most well-known and long-established are venues for the most celebrated of visitors from all over the world. Claridge's (Brook Street), perhaps London's most illustrious and discreet of *hôtels-de-luxe,* may often be seen flying the flag of some visiting monarch or president. Behind its red-brick exterior it remains imperturbably comfortable. Mr Claridge, who acquired the hotel shortly after it first opened in 1808, was quick to foster its reputation. By 1848, 'the year of revolutions' in Europe, he feared it might be difficult to accommodate the fugitive Pope Pius IX as he already had so many other royalties in residence. The Connaught (Carlos Place), arguably London's best hotel, is smaller, more intimate but equally luxurious: a favourite of Hollywood stars. Brown's (Dover Street), founded by the original Mr Brown, butler to Lord Byron, retains the character of a town home for the landed gentry. Franklin D Roosevelt honeymooned here with Eleanor; from here the Dutch government in exile declared war on the Japanese.

In 1985 the MAYFAIR Hotel (Stratton Street), with its own in-house theatre/cinema and reputation for fostering the performing arts, was the first British hotel to receive a satellite TV link.

Above: Something of the original May Fair atmosphere lingers today in the alleyways of Shepherd Market. Right: MAYFAIR's Savile Row has become a synonym across the world for the best in gentlemen's tailoring.

Shopping The shops of MAYFAIR testify to the area's elegance and wealth. Savile Row, together with its surrounds, is home to the world's finest gentlemen's tailors. Its clients have ranged from Mick Jagger to Fred Astaire, from Elton John to John Kennedy. The 180m Burlington Arcade, perhaps London's finest arcade built in 1819, is famous for expensive gifts. In 1828 its seventy-two shops were let at an annual rent of £18 to a variety of merchants, including a bookseller, glovers, a goldsmith, hairdressers, hatters, hosiers, jewellers, milliners, an optician, shoemakers, tobacconists and a wine maker, all offering sheltered facilities for 'the leisurely and agreeable spending of money.'

The **Royal Institution**, Grafton Street, was founded in 1799 for the 'promotion, diffusion and extension of scientific knowledge'. Among a dazzling array of scientists who have lectured here have been the chemist Sir Humphry Davy and his assistant Michael Faraday.

Shepherd Market, south of Curzon Street, is a picturesque labyrinth of narrow roads and alleyways lined with smart souvenir shops and pavement cafés – whose patrons can watch passing prostitutes peddle their wares while first-floor curtains semaphore their curious codes. With its tiny market-place, its atmospheric, bow-windowed Shepherd's Tavern, its bizarrely-named Tiddy Dol's eating house (after the local 18thC gingerbread maker), Shepherd Market retains its unique links with the outlawed May Fair. Today, surrounded by more opulent streets, this impudent village quarter remains the cultural heart of lofty MAYFAIR.

Famous People

George Fredrick Händel (1685-1759), celebrated German-English composer, lived at #25 Brook Street – where he wrote the *Messiah* and perished.

Clive of India (1725-74), brilliant soldier and administrator who built the foundations of the British Empire in India, bought #45 Berkeley Square c1763. Here he died from an overdose of laudanum (tincture of opium) – thought to have been suicide while in a state of acute depression.

John Adams (1735-1826), later second President of the United States but then the first American minister to Britain, occupied #9 Grosvenor Square from 1785.

Two French kings, **Louis XVIII** (1755-1824) & **Charles X** (1757-1836), lodged in South Audley Street.

Elizabeth II, Queen of the United Kingdom and Head of the Commonwealth, was born in MAYFAIR's Bruton Street. She is seen here in 1973 taking the salute at her official birthday ceremony, Trooping the Colour, in WHITEHALL.

Thomas Cubitt (1788-1855), the energetic and first 'speculative builder' who remodelled much of Mayfair, invented the concept of the modern civil engineering company. Born the son of a carpenter, Cubitt was nicknamed 'the Eperor of the Building Trade' and died a very wealthy man.

Bertie Wooster occupied a house in Half Moon Street with his famous man-servant **Jeeves.**

George Joseph Smith (1872-1915), the 'brides in the bath' murderer, married the first of the three wives he drowned at St George's Hanover Square. From his homicidal business-venture he made a total gain of £3,500 before his eventual conviction and execution.

Norman Parkinson (b1913), jet-setting pioneer fashion photographer who made 'moving pictures with a still camera', set up his first studio at #1 Dover Street in 1934. To his MAYFAIR doors, open until 2am on Court nights, came a flock of tremulous young debutantes and mothers after late-night presentations at Buckingham Palace.

Queen Elizabeth II (b1926) was born at #17 Bruton Street on 21 April. The original house has since been demolished.

Other more recent residents of MAYFAIR have included the politicians **Lord Boothby** and **Enoch Powell**, the cartoonist **Sir Osbert Lancaster**, the actor **Lawrence Olivier** and the novelist **C P Snow**.

THE BANK

The MONOPOLY BANK is allotted no square on the MONOPOLY board. No symbol of office announces its presence. Yet its influence in the game is all-pervading. The BANK issues banknotes and pays salaries; it holds Title Deeds and sells them; it controls building and it auctions Sites; it loans funds on mortgages and supervises bankruptcies; it collects taxes, fines, financial penalties and interest payments. Above all, its resources are limitless, for the BANK can never run out of funds.

The Bank of England is MONOPOLY London's bank *par excellence*: banker to the Government; banker to British and overseas banks; manager of the National Debt; administrator of Exchange Control Regulations; issuer of banknotes; supervisor of the banking system; custodian of the nation's gold reserves; and lender of last resort. Like the MONOPOLY BANK its influence is everywhere. It occupies a 1.6ha site at the corner of Threadneedle Street and Princes Street, nearly 1km east of St Paul's Cathedral. This spot – one of the City of London's most congested intersections where seven major roads converge – is known simply as 'Bank'. In the immediate vicinity are the Stock Exchange, the Royal Exchange, the Mansion House, the 'big four' commercial banks and the great foreign financial houses. This is London's financial heart – the premier financial centre in the world.

The Bank of England is at the hub of a City collage, surrounded by great financial landmarks like the Stock Exchange, Lloyd's insurance market and the National Westminster Tower.

It was at the prompting of a shrewd Scot in the reign of Dutch-born William III that the Bank of England was founded by Act of Parliament and Royal Charter. In 1694 wealthy City merchant William Paterson – a buccaneering and colourful financier who had travelled widely in Europe and the West Indies – perceived the British Government's cash deficiency caused by the wars with France as an ideal opportunity to realise his dream of a national bank. Within a short time a loan capital of £1,200,000 had been raised by public subscription and lent to the Government at an annual interest of eight percent, plus £4,000 'management expenses' – yielding for the new venture a guaranteed income of £100,000 yearly.

Despite its somewhat nomadic existence until 1734, the Bank of England soon became accepted as part of the Establishment, internationally respected for the integrity and industry of its officers – notwithstanding sardonic Tory cries of 'Dutch finance', for the new institution was modelled on Amsterdam's existing central bank and heavily supported by Dutch investors. In common with its highly active competitors the Bank was

Sir John Soane (1753-1837), appointed acrchitect to the Bank of England in 1788, was knighted in 1831 and bequeathed to the nation his house, now Sir John Soane's Museum, at #13 Lincoln's Inn Fields, WC2.

originally permitted to issue banknotes only to the value of its capital, until, in 1708, the Government restricted the right of other banks to issue notes, thus creating for the Bank of England an effective monopoly. Yet the first fixed notes – for £20, £30, £40, £50 and £100 – were not issued until 1725.

Then, in 1734, the Bank decamped from Grocer's Hall to its more permanent and present location in Threadneedle Street where, in 1780, it survived the assault of the Gordon Rioters with the help of a hastily summoned military detachment – the 'Bank Picquet' which subsequently lingered until 1973. In 1788 one of the most brilliant architects in Europe, the bricklayer's son Sir John Soane, was appointed to the Bank. By 1801 he had created a large, single-storeyed, Portland stone structure of unique grace. The oldest remaining part of the Bank – its massive, secure, windowless curtain walls relieved only by perfectly proportioned Corinthian columns – dates from this period. But of the rest of Soane's masterwork little remains, following reconstruction in 1921-37. Nikolaus Pevsner is scathing: 'To preserve the screen-wall only and scoop out all the rest strikes

With the Greenwich Meridian only a few miles downstream, the City of London's strategic location between the time-zones of East and West ensures its continued pre-eminence as the world's number one banking and financial centre.

one as peculiarly distasteful . . .' Hubert Baker's inter-war creation is a dominant massif extending seven storeys up and three down.

The Bank of England remained a private company until 1946 when it was nationalised by a post-war socialist government – realising for the first time William Paterson's concept of a truly national bank. Now the National Debt – which in William III's reign was only slightly more than one million pounds – stands at over £140,000,000,000; while in early 1987 gold and foreign currency reserves reached more than £21,000,000,000.

Today the Bank of England is among the oldest of the world's central banks. Yet its traditional gatekeepers and messengers, who move elegantly about in pink tails and scarlet waistcoats, belie a sophisticated world of high finance and international powermongering that makes the 'Old Lady of Threadneedle Street' one of the foremost banks, and the City of London the foremost international banking centre, on earth.

PART 2

The spaces of the MONOPOLY board cover the panorama of central London. From the OLD KENT ROAD south of the Thames to KINGS CROSS STATION in the north, from the East End's WHITECHAPEL ROAD to PARK LANE in the West End — they pilot the traveller through a kaleidoscope of city life. Here he will experience the tiny cul-de-sac of VINE STREET, the power-packed avenue of WHITEHALL, the bustling department stores of OXFORD STREET, the openness of TRAFALGAR SQUARE, the City atmosphere at FENCHURCH ST STATION, and the select exclusivity of an entire district in MAYFAIR. To tour this kaleidoscope is to see and understand London at all its levels. Yet such a tour may take many forms. It may be partially or wholly on foot, or by car, bus or tube. It can include a river trip. It may be accomplished in a day or a week — a limited or a comprehensive tour.

To tour the streets of London in their order on the MONOPOLY board is possible but impracticable, involving as it would much back-tracking and repetition. In addition, many places of general interest may be passed while travelling from one MONOPOLY space to another. To prepare a detailed route would be rigid and restricting; yet to set off without some form of itinerary can be confusing and time-wasting. The following pages therefore list five suggested routes which together cover the whole of MONOPOLY London, with places of interest listed in approximate geographical order. The tourist may follow these routes at his discretion, perhaps using them to prepare his own tour, or dipping into them to select streets or items of particular interest to himself.

Places of interest mentioned in Part 1 are indicated thus (open to the public) or thus (closed to the public or no longer standing). Other places of interest nearby or *en route* to or from the relevant MONOPOLY space are also listed, but with no symbol. Telephone numbers are given for attractions which are open to the public at certain times (excluding public houses, theatres, shops etc which may be visited during standard opening hours).

Route I
South of the Thames

ELECTRIC COMPANY
(Tube: Vauxhall)
Battersea Power Station [Battersea Park Road, SW8]
(Conversion to Battersea Leisure Centre due for completion early-1990s.)

Battersea Park Funfair

OLD KENT ROAD (SE1, SE15)
(Tube: London Bridge/New Cross Gate)
North Peckham Civic Centre [#168/tel 01-703-6311]
Thomas à Becket [#320]
Livesey Museum [#682/tel 01-639-5604]

Greenwich (SE10)
Cutty Sark [King William Walk/tel 01-858-3445]
Gipsy Moth IV
National Maritime Museum [Romney Road, SE10/tel 01-858-4422]

WATER WORKS
Thames Barrier [Unity Way, SE10/tel 01-854-1373]
(May also be approached by river — services from central London.)

South of the Thames
ROUTE I
Camden Road
Camden Town
CAMDEN
NORTH LONDON LINE- BR
Essex Road
A1
London Fields
Mornington Crescent
St. Pancras
Euston
Great Portland Street
Euston Square
Warren Street
Russell Square
CLERKENWELL
Old Street
Bethnal Green
Shoreditch
Whitechapel
BLOOMSBURY
Farringdon
Moorgate
Liverpool Street
Goodge Street
Chancery Lane
Barbican
Holborn Viaduct
THE CITY
Aldgate East
Tottenham Court Road
Holborn
Snow Hill Tunnel Open 1988
St. Pauls
DLR
Bank
Aldgate
Fenchurch Street
Shadwell
Oxford Circus
SOHO
Covent Garden
Aldwych
Temple
Blackfriars
Mansion House
Cannon Street
Tower Hill
Tower Gateway
MAYFAIR
Leicester Square
Piccadilly Circus
Monument
LONDON BRIDGE
WAPPING
Wapping
Charing Cross
Embankment
TOWER BRIDGE
A200
London Bridge
Waterloo
St. James's Park
Westminster
Borough
BERMONDSEY
St. James's Park
Lambeth North
Elephant & Castle
WESTMINSTER
Victoria
A215
A3
South Bermondsey
A2
OLD KENT ROAD
Pimlico
Kennington
A3212
Vauxhall
WALWORTH
Kennington Park
Oval
Battersea Power Station
Battersea Park
CAMBERWELL
Queen's Road, Peckham
Queenstown Road, Battersea
PECKHAM
Stockwell
Peckham Rye
Denmark Hill
Wandsworth Road
Loughborough Junction
Ruskin Park
Clapham
Clapham North
CLAPHAM
Brixton
A3
East Dulwich
Peckham Rye Park
Clapham Common
North Dulwich
Herne Hill
A23
Brockwell Park
DULWICH
Dulwich Park
Balham
West Dulwich
Tulse Hill
A215
Streatham Hill
Sydenham Hill
West Norwood
STREATHAM
Sydenham

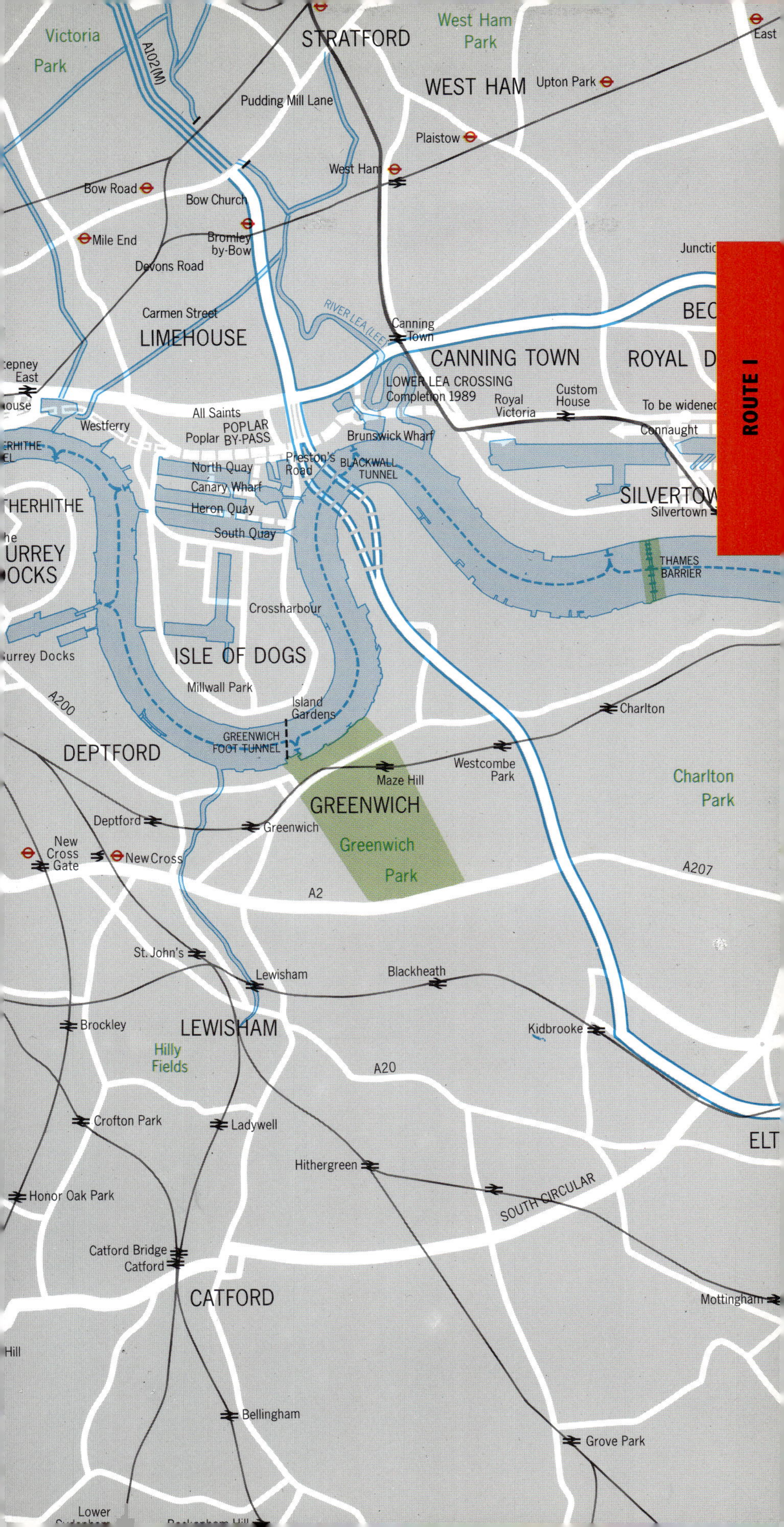

Victoria Park
STRATFORD
West Ham Park
WEST HAM
Upton Park
East
A102(M)
Pudding Mill Lane
Plaistow
West Ham
Bow Road
Bow Church
Mile End
Bromley by-Bow
Devons Road
Carmen Street
LIMEHOUSE
RIVER LEA (LEE)
Canning Town
CANNING TOWN
ROYAL D
Junctio
BEC
LOWER LEA CROSSING
Completion 1989
Royal Victoria
Custom House
To be widened
Connaught
ROUTE I
Westferry
All Saints
POPLAR BY-PASS
Poplar
Brunswick Wharf
North Quay
Canary Wharf
Heron Quay
South Quay
Preston's Road
BLACKWALL TUNNEL
SILVERTOW
Silvertown
THAMES BARRIER
THERHITHE
URREY OCKS
Crossharbour
ISLE OF DOGS
urrey Docks
Millwall Park
Island Gardens
A200
GREENWICH FOOT TUNNEL
DEPTFORD
Charlton
Westcombe Park
Maze Hill
Charlton Park
GREENWICH
Greenwich Park
Deptford
Greenwich
New Cross Gate
New Cross
A2
A207
St. John's
Lewisham
Blackheath
Brockley
LEWISHAM
Kidbrooke
Hilly Fields
A20
Crofton Park
Ladywell
ELT
Hithergreen
SOUTH CIRCULAR
Honor Oak Park
Catford Bridge
Catford
CATFORD
Mottingham
Hill
Bellingham
Grove Park
Lower

Route 2
City and stations

IN JAIL
(Tube: Tower Hill)
- The Tower of London [Tower Hill, EC3/tel 01-709-0765]
  - Bloody Tower
  - Bell Tower
  - Traitor's Gate
  - Tower Green
  - Queen's House
  - Tower Hill
  - Martin Tower
  - Crown Jewels
  - White Tower

Tower Bridge [Tower Bridge Road, SE1]
  Tower Bridge Walkway

City wall remains [behind Tower Hill tube station]

FENCHURCH S^T STATION [Railway Place, EC3]
(Tube: Tower Hill)
- Station architecture

World Trade Centre [St Katherine's Way, E1/tel 01-488-2400]

GO TO JAIL
(Tube: Wapping)
- Metropolitan Police Historical Museum [Wapping] — open early-1990s

WHITECHAPEL ROAD (E1)
(Tube: Aldgate East/Whitechapel)
- Sidney Street
- The Blind Beggar [#337]
- London Hospital
- Booth House [#153/175]
- Whitechapel Bell Foundry [#32/34/tel 01-247-2599] — open only by prior arrangement
- Whitechapel Art Gallery [#80/82 Whitechapel High Street/tel 01-377-0107]

Petticoat Lane market [Middlesex Street, E1]

LIVERPOOL S^T STATION (Liverpool Street, EC2)
(Tube: Liverpool Street)
- Station architecture
- Broad Street leisure complex

THE BANK
(Tube: Bank)
- The Bank of England [Princes Street/Threadneedle Street, EC2]

Mansion House [Bank, EC2]
The Royal Exchange [Threadneedle Street/Cornhill, EC3]
The Stock Exchange [Capel Court, EC2]
National Westminster Tower [Bishopsgate, EC2]
Lloyd's Building [Leadenhall Street, EC3]

GO
(Tube: St Paul's/Barbican)
The London Museum [London Wall, EC2/tel 01-600-3699]

Barbican Centre for Arts and Conferences [Barbican, EC2/tel 01-638-4141]

St John's Gate [St John's Lane, EC1/tel 01-253-6644]
St John's Crypt [St John's Square, EC1] — entrance only via St John's Gate

THE ANGEL ISLINGTON (N1)
(Tube: Angel)
The Angel [Co-op Bank, #1 Islington High Street]
Camden Passage Antique Market
Chapel Street Market
Business Design Centre [Upper Street/tel 01-359-3535]
Islington Green
Old Queen's Head Tavern [Essex Road]
Crown & Woolpack [St John Street]
Old Red Lion [St John Street]
Sadler's Wells Theatre [Rosebery Avenue/tel 01-278-6563]

PENTONVILLE ROAD (N1)
(Tube: Angel/King's Cross)
The Medici Society [#34/42/tel 01-837-7099]
Joseph Grimaldi Park [corner of Rodney Street]
Lenin's home [Vernon Rise, off Penton Rise]
Regents Canal [Caledonian Road, N1]

KINGS CROSS STATION (Euston Road, NW1)
(Tube: King's Cross)
Station architecture Great Northern Hotel

EUSTON ROAD (NW1)
(Tube: King's Cross/St Pancras/Euston/Euston Square/Warren Street)
St Pancras Station
Midland Grand Hotel/St Pancras Chambers
British Library
Shaw Theatre [#100]
Euston Station
Wellcome Institute [#183/tel 01-387-4477]
Thames Television [#306]
British Telecom Tower [Howland Street]
John F Kennedy statue [junction with Marylebone Road]

Madame Tussaud's [Marylebone Road, NW1/tel 01-935-6861]
London Planetarium [Marylebone Road, NW1/tel 01-486-1121]

MARYLEBONE STATION (Marylebone Road, NW1)
(Tube: Marylebone)
Station architecture
Hotel Great Central (now offices)

Regent's Park (NW1)

City and Stations
ROUTE 2
CAMDEN
Camden Town
London Zoo
REGENT'S PARK
Mornington Crescent
Euston
King's Cross
St. Pancras
Euston Tower
Warren Street
Great Portland Street
Regent's Park
Baker Street
Marylebone
BLOOMSBURY
SOHO
COVENT GARDEN
MAYFAIR
PICCADILLY CIRCUS
Charing Cross
HYDE PARK
GREEN PARK
ST. JAMES'S PARK
HYDE PARK CORNER
Buckingham Palace
Westminster
Westminster Abbey
Houses of Parliament
St. James's Park
WESTMINSTER
Victoria
PIMLICO
Pimlico
Vauxhall
THAMES
HAVERSTOCK HILL
ADELAIDE ROAD
ALBERT ROAD
PARKWAY
CAMDEN HIGH ST.
BAYHAM STREET
CAMDEN STREET
ROYAL COLLEGE ST.
ST. PANCRAS WAY
CROWNDALE RD.
PANCRAS ROAD
MIDLAND RD.
YORK WAY
CALEDONIAN ROAD
PARK VILLAGE EAST
OUTER CIRCLE
ALBANY STREET
HAMPSTEAD ROAD
EVERSHOLT STREET
EUSTON ROAD
MARYLEBONE ROAD
GLOUCESTER PLACE
BAKER STREET
PORTLAND PL.
GREAT PORTLAND STREET
TOTTENHAM COURT ROAD
GOWER STREET
WOBURN PLACE
RUSSELL SQUARE
SOUTHAMPTON ROW
GRAY'S INN ROAD
KING'S CROSS ROAD
THEOBALD'S ROAD
HOLBORN
HIGH HOLBORN
KINGSWAY
ALDWYCH
STRAND
MORTIMER ST.
WIGMORE STREET
OXFORD STREET
MARBLE ARCH
A5
PARK LANE
REGENT STREET
CHARING CROSS ROAD
SHAFTESBURY AVENUE
LEICESTER SQUARE
HAYMARKET
TRAFALGAR SQUARE
NORTHUMBERLAND AVENUE
EMBANKMENT
WATERLOO BRIDGE
PICCADILLY
ST. JAMES'S ST.
PALL MALL
THE MALL
WHITEHALL
VICTORIA EMBANKMENT
BELVEDERE RD.
YORK ROAD
CONSTITUTION HILL
KNIGHTSBRIDGE
BIRDCAGE WALK
WESTMINSTER BRIDGE
GROSVENOR PLACE
BELGRAVE SQUARE
SLOANE STREET
BROMPTON ROAD
BEAUCHAMP PLACE
PONT ST.
HOBART PL.
GROSVENOR GDNS
BUCKINGHAM PALACE ROAD
BUCKINGHAM GATE
TOTHILL STREET
BRESSENDEN PLACE
VICTORIA STREET
MARSHAM ST.
ABINGDON ST.
HORSEFERRY ROAD
LAMBETH BRIDGE
LAMBETH PALACE RD.
LAMBETH
SLOANE SQUARE
SLOANE AVENUE
EBURY STREET
VAUXHALL BRIDGE ROAD
BELGRAVE ROAD
MILLBANK
ALBERT EMBANKMENT
PIMLICO ROAD
EBURY BRIDGE RD.
CHELSEA BRIDGE RD.
KING'S ROAD
ROYAL HOSPITAL ROAD
EMBANKMENT
GROSVENOR ROAD
VAUXHALL BRIDGE
HARLEYFORD RD.
OAKLEY ST
PENTONVILLE

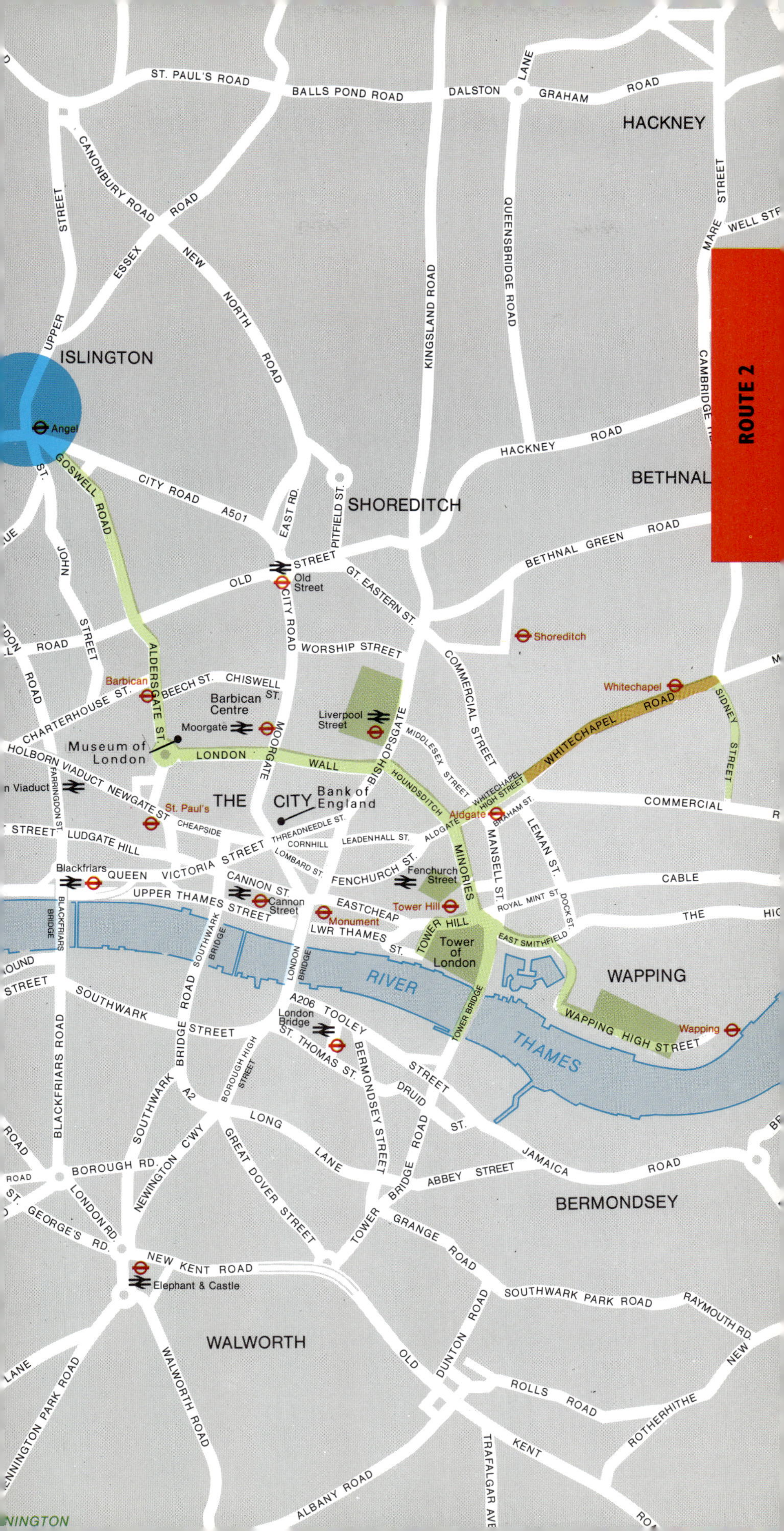

ROUTE 2
ISLINGTON
Angel
HACKNEY
SHOREDITCH
BETHNAL
THE CITY
WAPPING
BERMONDSEY
WALWORTH
Barbican
Barbican Centre
Moorgate
Museum of London
Liverpool Street
Old Street
Shoreditch
Whitechapel
Aldgate
St. Paul's
Bank of England
Blackfriars
Cannon Street
Monument
Fenchurch Street
Tower Hill
Tower of London
London Bridge
Wapping
Elephant & Castle
RIVER THAMES

Route 3
Government, justice and commerce

TRAFALGAR SQUARE (WC2, SW1)

(Tube: Charing Cross)
- Nelson's Column/lions/fountains
- Norwegian Christmas Tree
- Trafalgar Square Police Station
- British Standard Measurements

George IV statue
James II statue
- National Gallery [tel 01-839-3321]
  - *Toilet of Venus* (Velazquez)

National Portrait Gallery [#2 St Martin's Place/tel 01-930-1552]
- Charing Cross

STRAND (WC2)

(Tube: Charing Cross/Aldwych)
- York Watergate [Watergate Walk]

Adelphi Theatre
Strand Palace Hotel
- Queen's Chapel of the Savoy [Savoy Street]
- Savoy Theatre [Savoy Court]
- Savoy Hotel [Savoy Court]

Lyceum Dance Hall [Wellington Street]
- St Mary-le-Strand

Gladstone statue
Dr Samuel Johnson statue
Roman Bath [Strand Lane/tel 01-798-2063/4]
King's College London
- St Clement Danes

INCOME TAX

(Tube: Aldwych)
- Somerset House [Lancaster Place, WC2]

BOW STREET (WC2)

(Tube: Covent Carden)
- Bow Street Police Station/Magistrates' Court [#28]
- Royal Opera House [tel 01-240-1200]
- Covent Garden Market
- Church of St Paul Covent Garden
- Theatre Royal Drury Lane

FREE PARKING

(Tube: Covent Garden)
- London Transport Museum [Wellington Street, WC2/tel 01-379-6344]

FLEET STREET (EC4)

(Tube: Aldwych/Temple)
- Temple Bar
- Church of St Dunstan-in-the-West

Prince Henry's Room [#17]
- Inner Temple
- Middle Temple
- Temple Church
- Dr Johnson's House [#17 Gough Square/tel 01-353-3745]
- Ye Olde Cheshire Cheese [Wine Office Court]
- El Vino's [#47]
- Daily Express building [#121]
- Press Association [#85]
- Reuters [#85]
- Church of St Bride [Bride Lane]

Whitefriars Crypt [#30 Bouverie Street, EC4]

St Paul's Cathedral [St Paul's Churchyard, EC4]

- Victoria Embankment
  - Waterloo Pier
  - Cleopatra's Needle
  - Bazalgette statue

NORTHUMBERLAND AVENUE (WC2)
(Tube: Charing Cross/Embankment)
- Playhouse Theatre
- Sherlock Holmes public house [#10 Northumberland Street]
- Royal Commonwealth Society [#18/tel 01-930-6733]

WHITEHALL (SW1)
(Tube: Charing Cross/Westminster)
King Charles I statue
- Great Scotland Yard
- Horse Guards
- Horse Guards Parade
- St James's Park
- Banqueting House [tel 01-930-4179]
- Ministry of Defence [Horseguards Avenue]
  - Henry VIII's Wine Cellar — restricted opening
- Cenotaph
- #10 Downing Street
- Cabinet War Rooms [tel 01-930-6961]

SUPER TAX
(Tube: Westminster)
- Her Majesty's Treasury [Parliament Street, SW1]

Sir Winston Churchill statue [Parliament Square, SW1]

Buckingham Palace [The Mall, SW1]
The Mall [SW1]
Institute of Contemporary Arts [Nash House, The Mall, SW1/tel 01-930-0493]

PALL MALL (SW1)
(Tube: Charing Cross/Piccadilly Circus/Green Park)
- Duke of York Column [Waterloo Place]

Clubs
  - Athenaeum [#107]
  - Travellers' Club [#106]
  - Reform Club [#104]
  - Royal Automobile Club [#89]
  - Junior Carlton [#30]
  - Army and Navy Club [#36]
  - United Oxford and Cambridge University Club [#71]
- Nell Gwynne's house — site of [#79]
- Marlborough House
- St James's Palace
- Lancaster House [Stable Yard, St James's Palace]

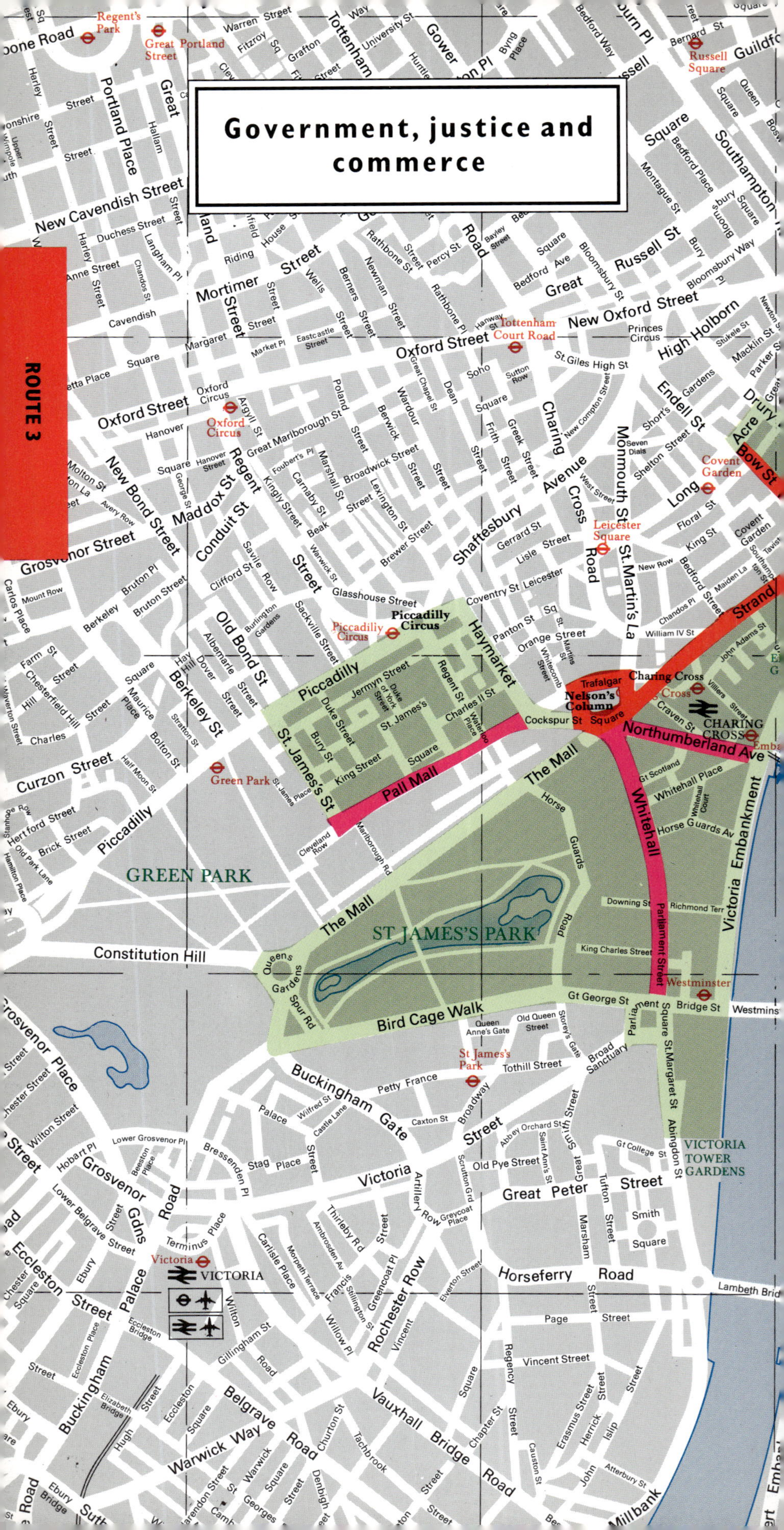

Government, justice and commerce
ROUTE 3
Regent's Park
Great Portland Street
Russell Square
Oxford Circus
Tottenham Court Road
Covent Garden
Leicester Square
Piccadilly Circus
Trafalgar
Nelson's Column
Square
Charing Cross
CHARING CROSS
Green Park
GREEN PARK
ST JAMES'S PARK
Westminster
St James's Park
Victoria
VICTORIA
VICTORIA TOWER GARDENS
Pall Mall
Whitehall
Parliament Street
Northumberland Ave
Strand
The Mall
Piccadilly
Haymarket
Constitution Hill
Bird Cage Walk
Horse Guards Road
Victoria Embankment
Oxford Street
New Oxford Street
Regent Street
Shaftesbury Avenue
Charing Cross Road
St James's Street
Victoria Street
Horseferry Road
Vauxhall Bridge Road
Buckingham Gate
Buckingham Palace Road
Grosvenor Place

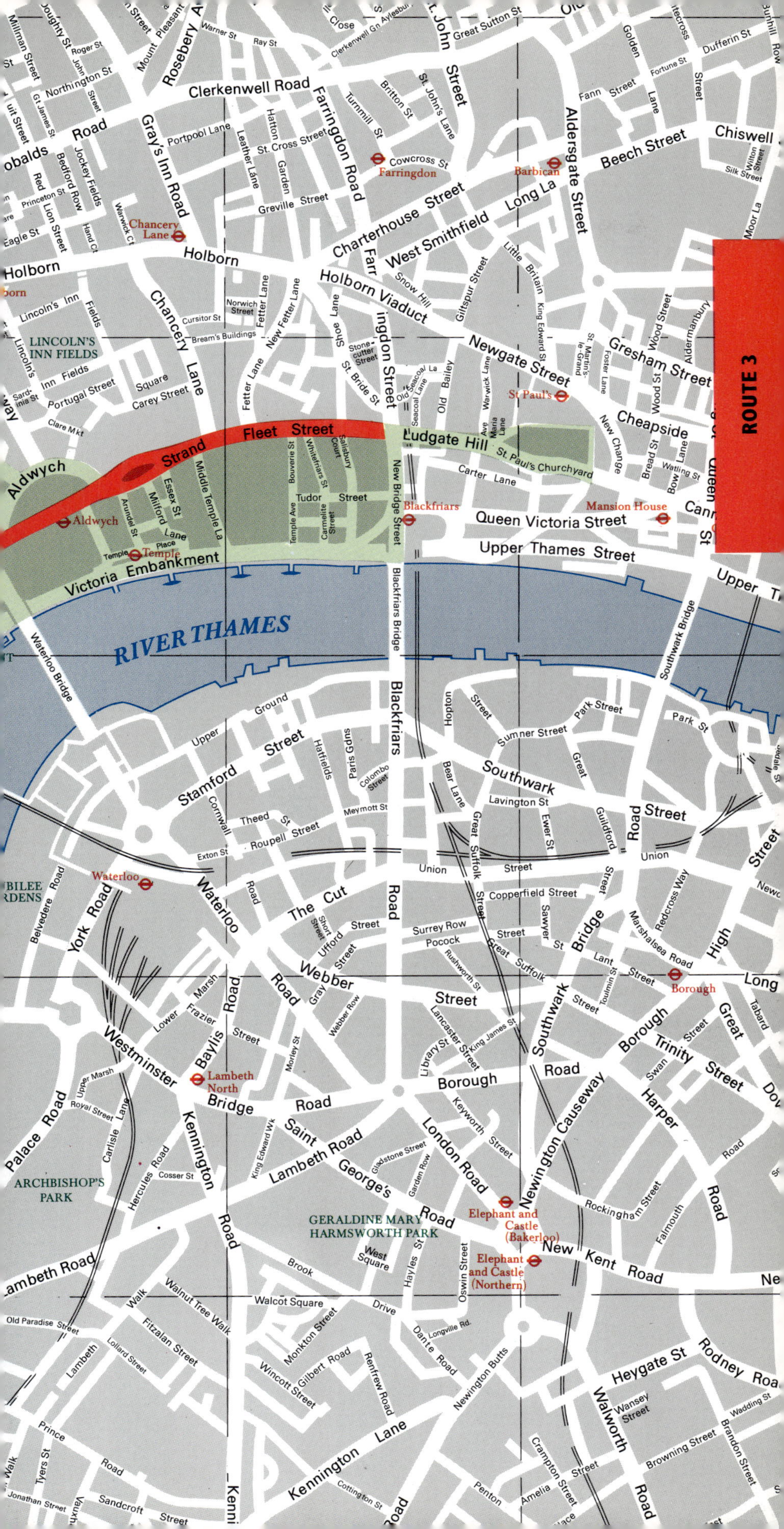

ROUTE 3
Clerkenwell Road
Farringdon Road
Gray's Inn Road
Rosebery Ave
Rogers St
Northington St
Warner St
Ray St
Mount Pleasant
Great Sutton St
St. John Street
St. John's Lane
Britton St
Turnmill St
Aylesbury St
Clerkenwell Gn
Golden Lane
Fortune St
Dufferin St
Fann Street
Whitecross Street
Chiswell Street
Silk Street
Wilson Street
Moor La
Beech Street
Aldersgate Street
Barbican
Long La
Cowcross St
Farringdon
Charterhouse Street
West Smithfield
Little Britain
King Edward St
Giltspur Street
Snow Hill
Holborn Viaduct
Holborn
Chancery Lane
Leather Lane
Hatton Garden
St. Cross Street
Greville Street
Portpool Lane
Theobalds Road
Jockey Fields
Bedford Row
Princeton St
Red Lion Street
Eagle St
Hand Ct
Warwick Ct
Gt. James St
Lincoln's Inn Fields
LINCOLN'S INN FIELDS
Portugal Street
Carey Street
Serle St
Sardinia St
Clare Mkt
Cursitor St
Norwich Street
Fetter Lane
New Fetter Lane
Bream's Buildings
Shoe Lane
Stonecutter Street
St. Bride St
Farringdon Street
Old Seacoal La
Seacoal Lane
Old Bailey
Warwick Lane
Ave Maria Lane
Newgate Street
St Paul's
St. Martin's-le-Grand
Foster Lane
Gresham Street
Wood Street
Aldermanbury
Cheapside
New Change
Bread St
Bow Lane
Watling St
Queen St
Cannon St
Aldwych
Strand
Fleet Street
Ludgate Hill
St. Paul's Churchyard
Carter Lane
Arundel St
Milford Lane
Essex St
Middle Temple La
Temple Place
Temple
Bouverie St
Whitefriars St
Salisbury Court
Tudor Street
Temple Ave
Carmelite Street
New Bridge Street
Blackfriars
Mansion House
Queen Victoria Street
Upper Thames Street
Victoria Embankment
RIVER THAMES
Waterloo Bridge
Blackfriars Bridge
Southwark Bridge
Upper Ground
Stamford Street
Hatfields
Paris Gdns
Colombo Street
Hopton Street
Sumner Street
Park Street
Park St
Southwark Street
Bear Lane
Great Suffolk Street
Lavington St
Ewer St
Guildford Street
Southwark Bridge Road
Union Street
Cornwall Road
Theed St
Roupell Street
Meymott St
Exton St
Waterloo
Waterloo Road
The Cut
Short Street
Ufford Street
Webber Street
Surrey Row
Pocock Street
Copperfield Street
Sawyer St
Redcross Way
Marshalsea Road
Lant Street
Toulmin St
Borough
Borough High Street
Long Lane
Tabard Street
Great Dover Street
Trinity Street
Swan Street
Harper Road
Rushworth St
Lancaster Street
King James St
Library St
Borough Road
Southwark Bridge Road
Blackfriars Road
Gray Street
Webber Row
Morley St
York Road
Belvedere Road
JUBILEE GARDENS
Lower Marsh
Frazier Street
Baylis Road
Westminster Bridge Road
Lambeth North
Upper Marsh
Royal Street
Carlisle Lane
Hercules Road
Cosser St
Kennington Road
King Edward Wk
Lambeth Road
Saint George's Road
Gladstone Street
Garden Row
London Road
Keyworth Street
Newington Causeway
Rockingham Street
Falmouth Road
Elephant and Castle (Bakerloo)
Elephant and Castle (Northern)
New Kent Road
GERALDINE MARY HARMSWORTH PARK
ARCHBISHOP'S PARK
Lambeth Palace Road
West Square
Hayles St
Oswin Street
Brook Drive
Walcot Square
Walnut Tree Walk
Lambeth Walk
Old Paradise Street
Fitzalan Street
Lollard Street
Wincott Street
Monkton Street
Gilbert Road
Renfrew Road
Dante Road
Longville Rd.
Newington Butts
Heygate St
Rodney Road
Wansey Street
Walworth Road
Wadding St
Brandon Street
Browning Street
Crampton Street
Amelia Street
Penton Place
Kennington Lane
Cottington St
Kennington Park Road
Prince's Road
Tyers St
Jonathan Street
Sandcroft Street
Vauxhall Walk

Route 4
Shopping and entertainment

PICCADILLY (W1)
(Tube: Green Park/Piccadilly Circus)
Green Park
Athenaeum Hotel [#116]
Park Lane Hotel [Brick Street]
Arts Council [#105]
Ritz Hotel
Burlington Arcade
Piccadilly Arcade
Royal Academy of Arts [Burlington House/tel 01-734-9052]
Albany
Fortnum & Mason [#181]
Hatchard's [#187]
Simpson's [#203]
Jermyn Street
Piccadilly Hotel
Cinecentre cinema
Piccadilly Circus
- Eros

COVENTRY STREET (W1)
(Tube: Piccadilly Circus)
London Pavilion
Design Centre [Haymarket]
Trocadero
- Guinness World of Records
- London Experience

Prince of Wales Theatre
Royal Angus Hotel [#39]
Café de Paris [#3]
Automobile Association [#5 New Coventry Street]
Premiere cinema [New Coventry Street]
Swiss Centre [New Coventry Street]

LEICESTER SQUARE (WC2)
(Tube: Leicester Square/Piccadilly Circus)
Leicester Square garden
- Shakespeare statue
- Charlie Chaplin statue

Empire cinema
Empire Ballroom
Prince Charles cinema [Leicester Place]
Warner West End cinema [Cranbourn Street]
Odeon cinema
Leicester Square cinema
Old Curiosity Shop [#10 Irving Street]
Beefsteak Club [#9 Irving Street]
Westminster Central Reference Library [St Martin's Street/tel 01-798-2036]

VINE STREET (W1)
(Tube: Piccadilly Circus)
Vine Street Police Station [#10]
Man-in-Moon Passage
Swallow Street
Piccadilly Place
- Vine public house

REGENT STREET (W1, SW1)
(Tube: Oxford Circus/Piccadilly Circus)
Carlton House Terrace
British Travel Centre [#12 Lower Regent Street/tel 01-839-2470]
Ceylon Tea Centre [#22 Lower Regent Street]

- Lillywhites [#24 Lower Regent Street]
- Regent Street Quadrant
- Café Royal [#68]
- Veeraswamy's [#99/101]

Shopping

- Aquascutum [#100]
- Garrard [#112]
- Austin Reed [#103/113]
- Hedges & Butler [#153]
- Burberry's [#165]
- Gered [#158]
- Mappin & Webb [#170]
- Hamleys [#188/196]
- Liberty [#210/220]
- Dickins & Jones [#224]

Boosey & Hawkes [#295]

Great MARLBOROUGH STREET (W1)

(Tube: Oxford Circus)

- Liberty & Company [#210/220 Regent Street]
- Coach & Horses public house [#1]
- Palladium House [#1/4 Argyll Street]
- The London Palladium [#8 Argyll Street]
- Little MARLBOROUGH STREET
- Carnaby Street
- Magistrates' Court [#21]
- Dog & Trumpet public house [#37]
- London College of Music [#47]

OXFORD STREET (W1)

(Tube: Tottenham Court Road/Oxford Circus/Bond Street/Marble Arch)

- Adam & Eve Court [opposite Poland Street]

Oxford Circus [junction with Regent Street]

Department stores

- British Homes Stores [#252]
- John Lewis [#278]
- D H Evans [#318]
- Debenhams [#334]
- Selfridges [#400]
- Marks & Spencer [#458]
- Littlewoods [#506]
- C & A [#501/519]

Cumberland Hotel [Marble Arch]

- Tyburn Gallows — site of [Marble Arch]

BOND STREET (W1)

(Tube: Bond Street/Green Park)

- Phillips [#7 Blenheim Street]

Fenwick's department store [#63 New Bond Street]

- Sotheby's [#34/35 New Bond Street]

Shopping

- St Laurent [#72 and #113 New Bond Street]
- Celine of Paris [Celine of Paris [#28 New Bond Street]
- Wildenstein [#147 New Bond Street]
- Hermes [#156 New Bond Street]
- Patek Philippe [#15 New Bond Street]
- Asprey [#165 New Bond Street]
- Karl Lagerfeld [#173 New Bond Street]
- Cartier [#175/6 New Bond Street]
- Loewe [Loewe [#25 Old Bond Street]
- Chanel [#26 Old Bond Street]
- Gucci [#27 Old Bond Street]
- Rayne [#16 Old Bond Street]
- Thomas Agnew & Son [#43 Old Bond Street]

Westbury Hotel [New Bond Street/Conduit Street]

Museum of Mankind [#6 Burlington Gardens/tel 01-437-2224]

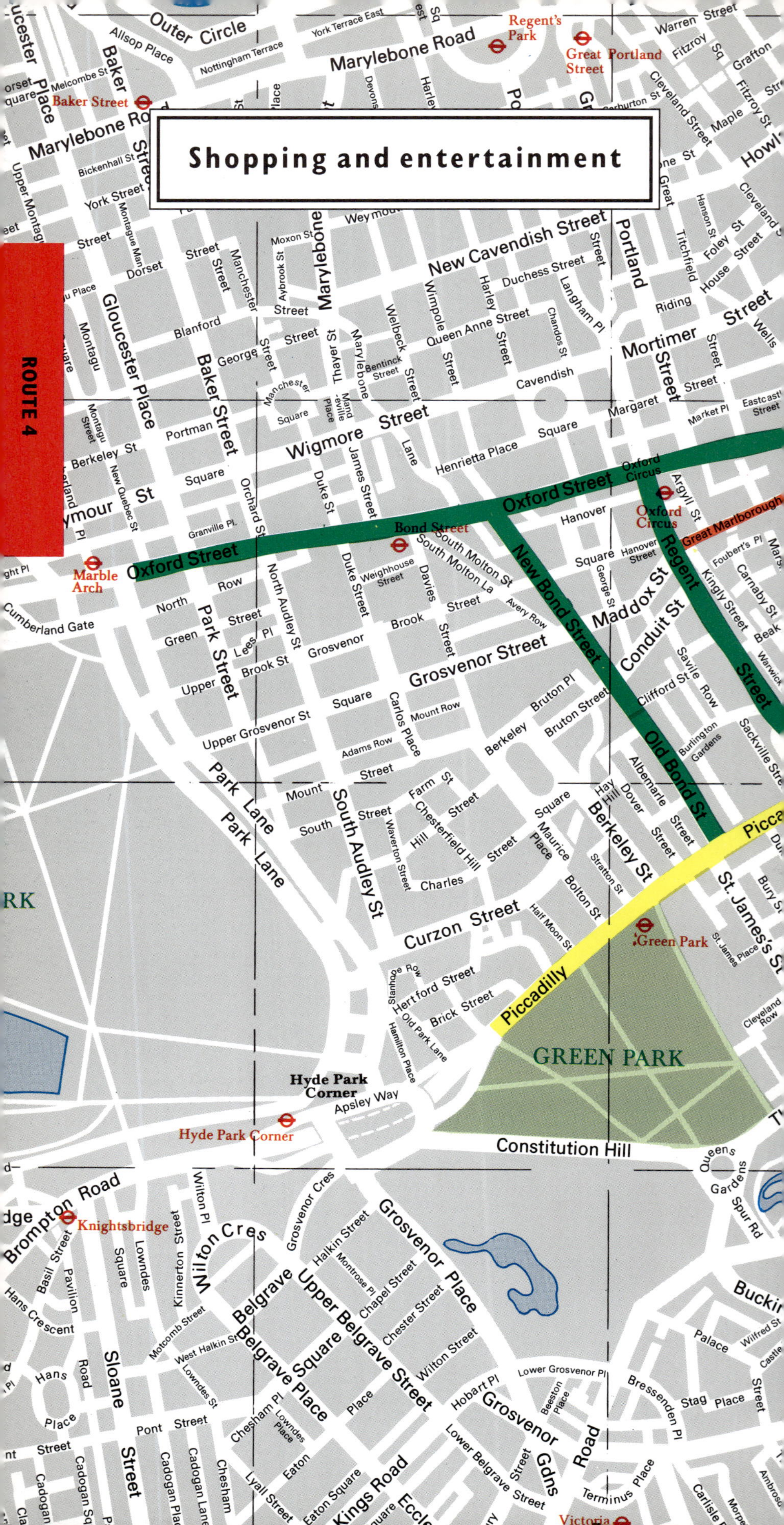

Shopping and entertainment
ROUTE 4
Outer Circle
Allsop Place
Nottingham Terrace
York Terrace East
Marylebone Road
Regent's Park
Great Portland Street
Warren Street
Fitzroy Sq
Grafton
Melcombe St
Baker Street
Gloucester Place
Dorset Square
Marylebone Road
Bickenhall St
York Street
Montague Mans
Cleveland Street
Maple
Fitzroy St
Howland
Carburton St
Great
Hanson St
Foley St
Titchfield
House Street
Cleveland
Weymouth
Moxon St
Aybrook St
Manchester Street
Marylebone
New Cavendish Street
Duchess Street
Harley Street
Langham Pl
Portland
Riding
Wells Street
Dorset Street
Blanford Street
Montagu Square
Montagu Street
George Street
Baker Street
Manchester Square
Thayer St
Marylebone Lane
Bentinck Street
Welbeck Street
Wimpole Street
Queen Anne Street
Chandos St
Cavendish Square
Mortimer Street
Margaret Street
Market Pl
Eastcastle Street
Portman Square
Wigmore Street
Mandeville Place
James Street
Duke St
Henrietta Place
Berkeley St
New Quebec St
Seymour St
Granville Pl.
Orchard St
Oxford Street
Oxford Circus
Argyll St
Hanover Square
Hanover Street
Great Marlborough
Bond Street
South Molton St
South Molton La
Marble Arch
North Row
Duke Street
Weighhouse Street
Davies Street
Brook Street
Avery Row
New Bond Street
George St
Maddox St
Conduit St
Regent Street
Kingly Street
Foubert's Pl
Carnaby St
Beak
Warwick
Cumberland Gate
North Row
Green Street
Park Street
Lees Pl
North Audley St
Upper Brook St
Grosvenor Square
Grosvenor Street
Savile Row
Clifford St
Upper Grosvenor St
Carlos Place
Mount Row
Bruton Pl
Bruton Street
Berkeley Square
Adams Row
Burlington Gardens
Sackville Street
Old Bond St
Park Lane
Mount Street
South Street
South Audley St
Farm St
Chesterfield Hill
Waverton Street
Hill Street
Charles Street
Hay Hill
Albemarle Street
Dover Street
Berkeley St
Stratton St
Maurice Place
Bolton St
Piccadilly
St. James's St
Bury St
PARK
Curzon Street
Half Moon St
Green Park
St. James's Place
Stanhope Row
Hertford Street
Brick Street
Old Park Lane
Hamilton Place
Cleveland Row
GREEN PARK
Hyde Park Corner
Apsley Way
Constitution Hill
Queens Gardens
Spur Rd
Brompton Road
Knightsbridge
Wilton Pl
Grosvenor Cres
Wilton Cres
Halkin Street
Grosvenor Place
Basil Street
Pavilion
Lowndes Square
Kinnerton Street
Montrose Pl
Chapel Street
Buckingham
Hans Crescent
Motcomb Street
Belgrave Square
Upper Belgrave Street
Chester Street
Wilton Street
Palace
Wilfred St
West Halkin St
Lowndes St
Belgrave Place
Castle
Hans Road
Sloane Street
Lower Grosvenor Pl
Bressenden Pl
Stag Place
Hobart Pl
Beeston Place
Grosvenor Gdns
Grosvenor Road
Hans Place
Pont Street
Chesham Pl
Lowndes Place
Eaton Place
Lower Belgrave Street
Cadogan Sq
Cadogan Place
Cadogan Lane
Chesham
Lyall Street
Eaton Square
Kings Road
Terminus Place
Carlisle Pl
Victoria

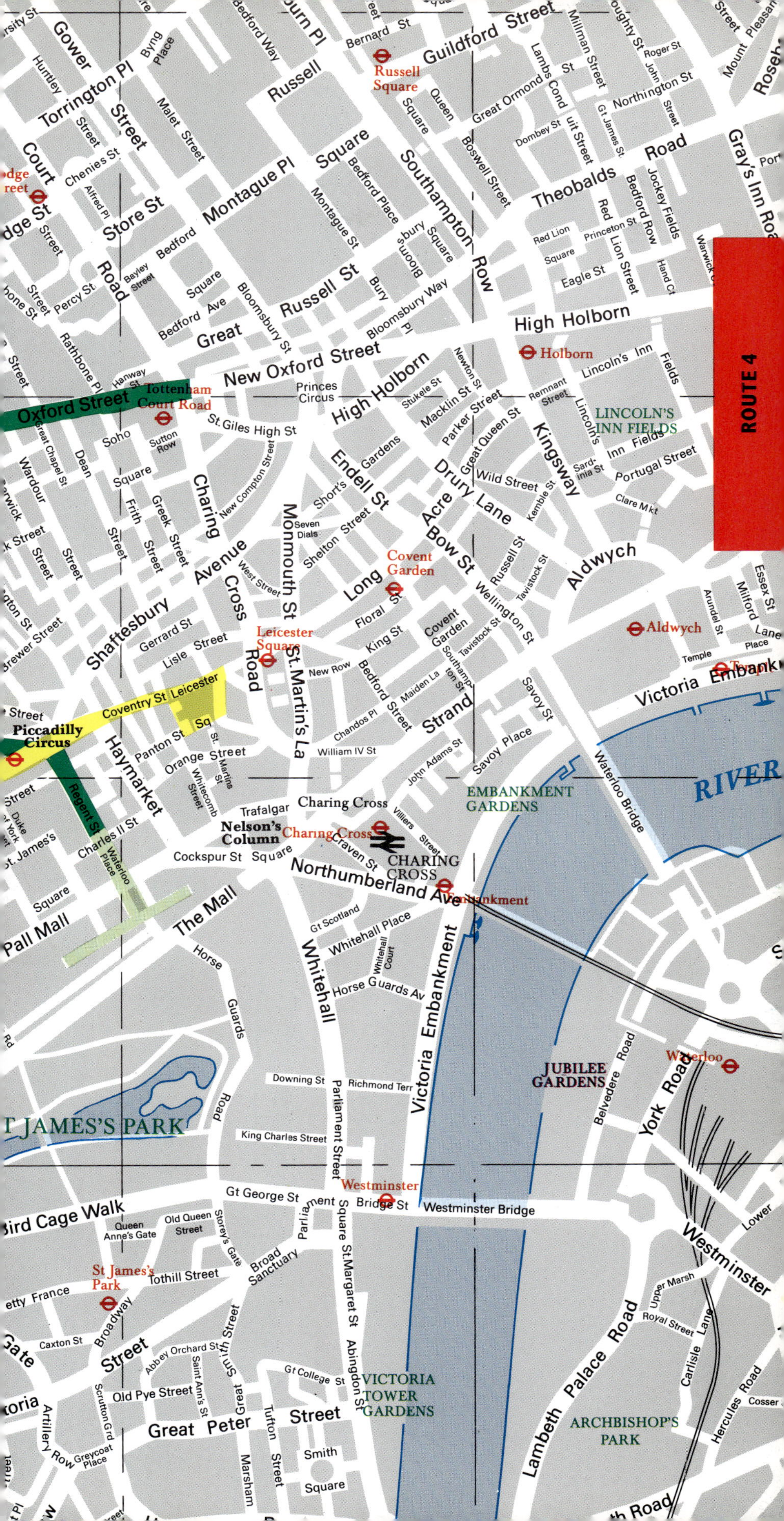

ROUTE 4
Gower Street
Huntley
Torrington Pl
Byng Place
Bedford Way
Russell Square
Bernard St
Guildford Street
Millman Street
Roger St
John Street
Northington St
Gray's Inn Road
Mount Pleasant
Malet Street
Chenies St
Alfred Pl
Store St
Montague Pl
Montague St
Bedford Place
Southampton Row
Queen Square
Great Ormond St
Lambs Conduit Street
Boswell Street
Dombey St
Gt James St
Theobalds Road
Bedford Row
Jockey Fields
Warwick Ct
Hand Ct
Red Lion Square
Red Lion Street
Princeton St
Eagle St
Bloomsbury Square
Bury Pl
Bloomsbury Way
Bloomsbury St
Russell St
Great Russell St
Bedford Ave
Bedford Square
Bayley Street
Percy St
Rathbone Pl
Hanway St
High Holborn
Holborn
Lincoln's Inn Fields
LINCOLN'S INN FIELDS
New Oxford Street
Princes Circus
Newton St
Remnant Street
Oxford Street
Tottenham Court Road
St Giles High St
Stukeley St
Macklin St
Parker Street
Great Queen St
Kingsway
Sardinia St
Portugal Street
Clare Mkt
Soho Square
Sutton Row
Dean Street
Great Chapel St
Wardour Street
Frith Street
Greek Street
Charing Cross Road
New Compton Street
Short's Gardens
Endell St
Drury Lane
Wild Street
Kemble St
Seven Dials
Monmouth St
Shelton Street
Long Acre
Bow St
Covent Garden
Russell St
Tavistock St
Aldwych
Essex St
Milford Lane
Arundel St
Temple Place
Temple
Shaftesbury Avenue
West Street
Gerrard St
Lisle Street
Leicester Square
Floral St
King St
Wellington St
Tavistock St
Southampton St
New Row
Bedford Street
Maiden La
Savoy St
Victoria Embankment
Coventry St
Leicester Sq
Piccadilly Circus
Haymarket
Panton St
Orange Street
St. Martin's Pl
Whitcomb Street
St. Martin's La
Chandos Pl
Strand
William IV St
John Adams St
Savoy Place
Waterloo Bridge
RIVER
EMBANKMENT GARDENS
Regent St
Charles II St
Trafalgar Square
Nelson's Column
Charing Cross
Villiers Street
Craven St
CHARING CROSS
Embankment
Northumberland Ave
St. James's Square
Waterloo Place
Cockspur St
Pall Mall
The Mall
Horse Guards Road
Gt Scotland
Whitehall Place
Whitehall Court
Whitehall
Horse Guards Av
Victoria Embankment
JUBILEE GARDENS
Belvedere Road
York Road
Waterloo
Downing St
Richmond Terr
Parliament Street
King Charles Street
Westminster
Gt George St
Bridge St
Westminster Bridge
Parliament Square
Bird Cage Walk
Queen Anne's Gate
Old Queen Street
Storey's Gate
Broad Sanctuary
St Margaret St
Westminster Bridge Road
Lower
Upper Marsh
Royal Street
Carlisle Lane
St James's Park
Tothill Street
Petty France
Broadway
Caxton St
Abbey Orchard St
Smith Street
Saint Ann's St
Gt College St
Abingdon St
VICTORIA TOWER GARDENS
Old Pye Street
Scrutton Grd
Artillery Row
Greycoat Place
Great Peter Street
Great Smith Street
Marsham Street
Tufton Street
Smith Square
Lambeth Palace Road
ARCHBISHOP'S PARK
Hercules Road
Cosser

Route 5
High life

PARK LANE (W1)
(Tube: Marble Arch/Hyde Park Corner)
- Marble Arch

Hotels
- Grosvenor House
- Dorchester
- Hilton
- Inn on the Park
- Londonderry
- Intercontinental

Royal Aeronautical Society [#4 Hamilton Place]
- Hyde Park Corner [SW1]
  - Apsley House [Wellington Museum/tel 01-499-5676]
  - Wellington statue
  - Wellington Arch
  - Royal Artillery Memorial
  - Machine Gun Corps Memorial
  - Lord Byron statue
  - Achilles statue

Hyde Park [W1, W2, SW7]
- Serpentine
- Speakers' Corner

MAYFAIR (W1)

(Tube: Bond Street/Green Park/Marble Arch/Hyde Park Corner)

- Grosvenor Square
  - United States Embassy
  - President Roosevelt statue
- Hanover Square
  - William Pitt statue
  - Church of St George Hanover Square [St George Street]
- Berkeley Square
  - Clermont Club — 'finest terrace house of London' [#44]

Shopping

- Savile Row
- Burlington Arcade

Cinemas and theatres

- Curzon cinema [Curzon Street]
- Gate Mayfair cinema [Stratton Street]
- Mayfair theatre [Stratton Street]

Museums and libraries

- Royal Institution [#21 Albermarle Street/tel 01-409-2992]
- Faraday Museum [#20 Albermarle Street/tel 01-409-2992]
- Mayfair Library [South Audley Street/tel 01-798-1391]

- Shepherd Market
  - Shepherd's Tavern [Hertford Street]
  - Tiddy Dol's [Hertford Street]
  - Ye Grapes [Shepherd Market]

Hotels

- Britannia Hotel [Grosvenor Square]
- Brown's [Dover Street]
- Claridge's [Brook Street]
- Connaught [Carlos Place]
- Curzon [Stanhope Row]
- Marriott Hotel [Grosvenor Square]
- Mayfair [Stratton Street]

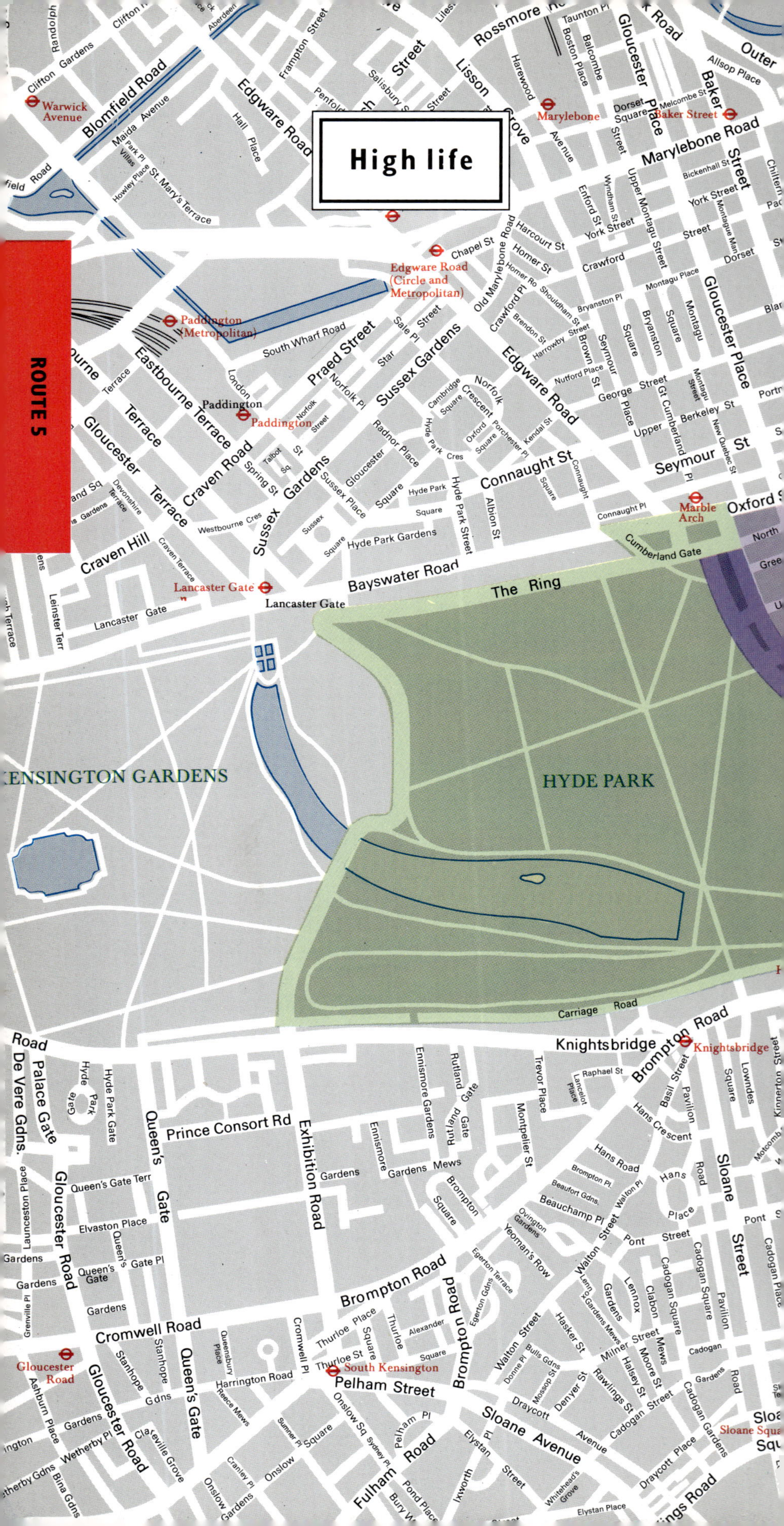

High life
ROUTE 5
Warwick Avenue
Blomfield Road
Clifton Gardens
Maida Avenue
Edgware Road
Hall Place
Frampton Street
Lisson Grove
Rossmore Road
Gloucester Place
Baker Street
Marylebone
Marylebone Road
Dorset Square
Allsop Place
Melcombe St
Harewood Avenue
Balcombe Street
Boston Place
Taunton Pl
St. Mary's Terrace
Park Pl Villas
Howley Place
Edgware Road (Circle and Metropolitan)
Chapel St
Old Marylebone Road
Harcourt St
Homer St
Crawford Street
York Street
Enford St
Wyndham St
Upper Montagu Street
Bickenhall St
Dorset Street
Montagu Place
Bryanston Square
Montagu Square
Bryanston Pl
Paddington (Metropolitan)
South Wharf Road
Praed Street
Sale Pl
Star Street
Sussex Gardens
Norfolk Crescent
Cambridge Square
Oxford Square
Hyde Park Crescent
Porchester Pl
Kendal St
Nutford Place
Brown St
Seymour Place
George Street
Gt Cumberland Pl
Upper Berkeley St
Seymour St
Connaught St
Connaught Square
Connaught Pl
Marble Arch
Oxford Street
Eastbourne Terrace
Gloucester Terrace
Craven Road
Paddington
London Street
Norfolk Pl
Spring St
Talbot Sq
Sussex Place
Radnor Place
Gloucester Square
Hyde Park Square
Hyde Park Street
Albion St
Hyde Park Gardens
Westbourne Cres
Craven Hill
Craven Terrace
Devonshire Terrace
Lancaster Gate
Leinster Terr
Bayswater Road
The Ring
Cumberland Gate
KENSINGTON GARDENS
HYDE PARK
Carriage Road
Knightsbridge
Brompton Road
Raphael St
Lancelot Place
Trevor Place
Montpelier St
Rutland Gate
Ennismore Gardens
Ennismore Gardens Mews
Exhibition Road
Prince Consort Rd
Queen's Gate
Hyde Park Gate
De Vere Gdns.
Palace Gate
Gloucester Road
Queen's Gate Terr
Elvaston Place
Queen's Gate Pl
Launceston Place
Grenville Pl
Cromwell Road
Stanhope Gdns
Harrington Road
Queensbury Place
Reece Mews
Cromwell Pl
Thurloe Place
Thurloe Square
Thurloe St
Alexander Square
South Kensington
Pelham Street
Pelham Pl
Onslow Square
Onslow Gardens
Sumner Pl
Sydney Pl
Fulham Road
Ashburn Place
Wetherby Pl
Clareville Grove
Cranley Pl
Bina Gdns
Egerton Terrace
Egerton Gdns
Yeoman's Row
Ovington Gardens
Beauchamp Pl
Beaufort Gdns
Brompton Sq
Hans Crescent
Hans Road
Hans Place
Basil Street
Pavilion Road
Sloane Street
Lowndes Square
Walton Street
Walton Pl
Pont Street
Lennox Gardens
Clabon Mews
Cadogan Square
Cadogan Place
Cadogan Gardens
Cadogan Street
Milner Street
Moore St
Halsey St
Hasker St
Rawlings St
Denyer St
Bulls Gdns
Mossop St
Draycott Avenue
Draycott Place
Sloane Avenue
Sloane Square
Elystan Pl
Elystan Street
Ixworth Pl
Whitehead's Grove
Elystan Place
Bury Walk
Pond Place

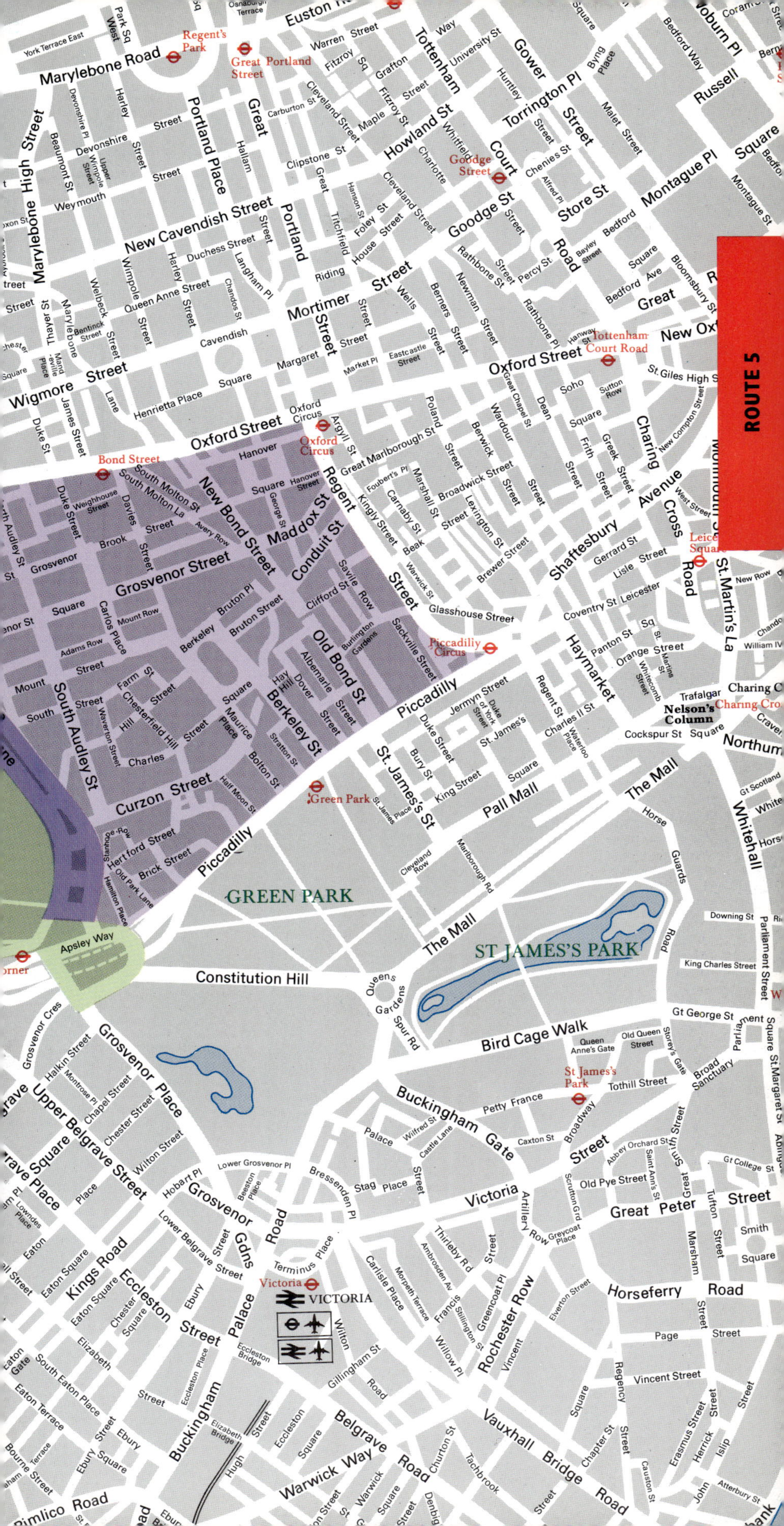

ROUTE 5
Regent's Park
Great Portland Street
Euston Road
Marylebone Road
Warren Street
Tottenham Court Road
Gower Street
Goodge Street
Torrington Pl
Russell Square
Montague Pl
Store St
Bedford Square
Marylebone High Street
Portland Place
New Cavendish Street
Weymouth Street
Devonshire Street
Mortimer Street
Wigmore Street
Cavendish Square
Oxford Street
Oxford Circus
Bond Street
Henrietta Place
Hanover Square
New Bond Street
Maddox St
Conduit St
Regent Street
Great Marlborough St
Carnaby St
Soho Square
Charing Cross Road
Shaftesbury Avenue
Grosvenor Street
Grosvenor Square
Berkeley Square
Berkeley St
Old Bond St
Piccadilly Circus
Piccadilly
South Audley St
Curzon Street
Green Park
Jermyn Street
St. James's St
Pall Mall
Haymarket
Leicester Square
Trafalgar Square
Charing Cross
Nelson's Column
Cockspur St
The Mall
Horse Guards Road
Whitehall
GREEN PARK
ST JAMES'S PARK
Constitution Hill
Apsley Way
Downing St
King Charles Street
Parliament Street
Bird Cage Walk
Queens Gardens
Spur Rd
Buckingham Gate
St James's Park
Tothill Street
Petty France
Broadway
Victoria Street
Great Peter Street
Old Pye Street
Horseferry Road
Grosvenor Place
Upper Belgrave Street
Chester Street
Wilton Street
Grosvenor Gdns
Buckingham Palace Road
Victoria
VICTORIA
Eccleston Street
Eaton Square
Kings Road
Rochester Row
Vincent Square
Vauxhall Bridge Road
Belgrave Road
Warwick Way
Pimlico Road

Illustration acknowledgements

By courtesy of the following organisations:
Alecto Historical Editions — 44.
BBC Hulton Picture Library — 37 above, 81, 84, 136 below, 175 below, 176.
Bridgeman Art Library — 61.
'Britain on View' (BTA/ETB) — 184.
British Library — 27, 115.
British Museum — 33, 41 above, 45, 73 above, 76, 130, 153 below, 160 above.
Communist Party Picture Library — 47 below.
Guildhall Library — 136 above, 178.
Imperial War Museum — 74.
Metropolitan Police Museum — 148, 149 above, 150.
Museum of London — 22, 23 above, 50 above, 53, 55 above, 56, 57, 96, 99 below, 102, 104 above, 107, 110, 114, 158, 160 below, 172.
National Army Museum — 90.
National Gallery — 99 above.
National Portrait Gallery — 30 right, 47 above, 50 below, 65 right, 69, 77, 78, 95 above, 95 below, 111, 116, 124, 133, 143, 155, 156, 166, 175 above.
National Railway Museum — 42.
Nigel Press Associates — 23 below.
Peter Jackson Collection — 66, 152.
PhotoSphere — 28 right, 34 left, 36, 52 left, 52 right, 121 right, 140 right, 159 below.
Post Office Archives — 35 above.
Press Association — 30 left, 39 above, 39 centre, 39 below, 185.
Rail Print, British Railways Board — 168.
Salvation Army — 37 below.
Sir John Soane's Museum — 188.
Visionbank — 10, 11, 12, 13, 14 above, 20 left, 21, 25 above, 25 below, 28 left, 29, 34 right, 35 below, 41 below, 46, 51, 55 below, 60, 62, 63, 65 left, 67, 68, 70, 71, 73 below, 75, 80, 83, 86, 87 left, 87 right, 92, 93 left, 93 right, 94, 97 left, 97 right, 98, 104 left, 104 right, 108, 109, 117 left, 117 right, 118, 121 left, 122, 123 left, 123 right, 127 left, 127 right, 128, 131, 132 above, 132 below, 135 left, 135 right, 137, 138, 140 left, 141, 142 left, 142 right, 146, 147, 149 below, 153 above, 154 left, 154 right, 159 above, 164, 165 left, 165 right, 169, 173 left, 173 right, 174 above, 174 left, 174 right, 179, 180, 181 left, 181 right, 182 above, 182 below, 187, 189. Contributing photographers for Visionbank are Tim Beddows, Keith Bernstein, Charles Bowman, Peter Cogram, Ray Daffurn, John Easterby, John Farnham, James Holmes, Neil Holmes, Peter Kowal, Tony Page, Bill Richards, Alyson Whalley, and Andy Williams.
John Waddington Ltd — 5, 14 below.

Select bibliography

Russell Ash *The Londoner's Almanac* Century 1985
Anthony Babington *A House in Bow Street* Macdonald 1969
F R Banks *The Penguin Guide to London* Penguin Books 1979
Felix Barker & Peter Jackson *London 2000 Years of a city and its people* MacMillan 1985
E T Benson *London Immortals* Wingate 1951
J Boswell *Life of Johnson* Dent 1901
Giles Brandreth *The Monopoly Omnibus* Willow 1985
H Clunn *The Face of London* Simpkin Marshall 1932
Peter Bushell *London's Secret History* Constable 1983
Randolph S Churchill *Winston S Churchill (Part II)* Heinemann 1969
Winston S Churchill *A History of the English-Speaking Peoples* Cassell 1956
Robert Clayton *Portrait of London* Robert Hale 1980
W R Dalzell *The Shell Guide to the History of London* Michael Joseph 1981
R S Dutton *London Homes* Wingate 1952
Sheila Fairfield *The Streets of London* MacMillan 1984
John Field *Place-names of Greater London* Batsford 1986
Ylva French *Blue Guide to London* A & C Black 1986
Alan A Jackson *London's Termini* David & Charles 1985
Michael Jackson *Pocket Guide to London* Mitchell Beazley 1983
Steve Jones *London the Sinister Side* Tragical History Tours Publications 1986
ed E K Kendall *Source-Book of English History* MacMillan 1907
ed Robert Latham *The Illustrated Pepys* Bell & Hyman 1985
A Lejeune & M Lewis *The Gentlemen's Clubs of London* Macdonald & Janes 1979
Arthur Mee *London: the City and Westminster* Hodder & Stoughton 1975
PC John Moore (article) *Bow Street*
H V Morton *Ghosts of London* Methuen 1941
Michael Nathenson & Doris Long *London Without Tears* Grafton Books 1986
Sir Nikolaus Pevsner *The Cities of London and Westminster* Penguin Books 1973
Anthony Sampson *Anatomy of Britain Today* Hodder & Stoughton 1966
J Strype *Stow's Survey* 1720
ed James Sutherland *The Oxford Book of Literary Anecdotes* 1976
G W Thornbury *Old and New London* Cassell, Petter & Galpin 1873
Malcolm Todd *Roman Britain 55BC-AD400* Fontana 1981
Geoffrey Trease *London A Concise History* Thames & Hudson 1975
Richard Trench & Ellis Hillman *London under London* John Murray 1985
Benjamin Vincent *Haydn's Dictionary of Dates* Moxon 1876
ed Benjamin Vincent *A Dictionary of Biography* Ward Lock 1877
ed Ben Weinreb & Christopher Hibbert *The London Encyclopædia* MacMillan 1985
John Wittich *Discovering London Villages* Shire Publications 1986
Encyclopædia Brittanica
Fodor's Fun in London Fodor 1985
Fodor's London 1986 Fodor 1986
The Guinness Book of Records
London Night Life Robert Nicholson 1984
Survey of London Greater London Council
Where's Where Eyre Methuen 1974

Index

Streets and other spaces on the MONOPOLY board are shown in capitals.
The symbol ◊ indicates either an illustration/map or a passing reference in a related illustration caption.
The letter R indicates an entry in the MONOPOLY Routes section; thus R5: 208 refers to Route 5 on page 208.

A

B

C

H

I

J

K

L

M

N

O

P

Q

R

S

T

U

V

W

Y